The Ultimate
Mental Toughness Guide:
Junior Roller Derby

Naomi "Sweetart" Weitz

ISBN:069275475X
ISBN-13:9780692754757

DEDICATION

This is book is dedicated to the INRD Pixies.

ACKNOWLEDGMENTS

Cover Photo: Molotov Cupcake, Age 12, Skating 2 years. Photo by Keli Burch-Moran
Back Cover Photo: Daisy Juke, Age 15, Skating 4 years. Photo by Cory Lund Photography.

Thank you to the Inland Northwest Derby Pixies for letting me crash your practices for interviews, yoga and skating. Thank you to all the photographers who let me include your art in this book: Cory Lund Photography, Eric Lyons Photography, Danny Ngan Photography, Lydia Brewer Photography, Diane Palmer, Dani Hubbard and Daisy Norris.
Thank you to my kids—for everything, always.

CONTENTS

 1 INTRODUCTION

Roller derby is awesome. You get to roller skate. You get to be tough. You get to make tons of new friends. You get to go on road trips and have sleepovers in hotel rooms. You get to have a cool alter-ego name. You get to compete and have the thrill of success. You get to do all those fun things while also pushing yourself to do some incredibly difficult things. That is what makes roller derby so awesome—it's exciting but also challenging.

Roller derby can be a welcome refuge for those seeking an alternative to the typical sports—volleyball, basketball, soccer, softball, etc. For many of you, it's the first team sport you've been involved with, or the first sport ever. For others, derby is a new and exciting platform to further develop athletic skills you began building in other areas such as speed skating, ice hockey or figure skating. Whatever path brought you to roller derby, now that you're here you probably want to give it your all.

"Roller derby is my life. It's probably the best thing that's ever happened to me. I didn't really have any friends or anything that was really me except my music. I created a separate family and we bond over everything. I don't even call them friends anymore, I call them my derby family."

—Blackheart Blockher

Age 14, Skating 4 years

The physical training involved with being your best in roller derby is tremendously demanding. The mental demands can be even bigger. Do you need help figuring out your roller derby goals? Do you know why you are doing this crazy, amazing sport? Have emotions such as anger, fear or frustration got in the way of your roller derby performance? Have you ever felt like you couldn't get out of your head? Have self-doubts overwhelmed you? Have you skated worse in games than at practice? Do you struggle with getting along with your teammates? Have you wanted to do all you can to be the very best derby skater you can be? If you answered 'yes' to any of these questions, this book is for you!

What Can This Mental Toughness Guide Do For You?

This book will help you to:

- Commit to your goals
- Be mindful
- Have fun
- Be focused
- Be consistent
- Perform your best

- Be confident
- Get out of your comfort zone
- Be a great teammate
- Build your character
- Do some yoga!

Roller derby can bring out your best but can also showcase your worst. You decide!

What Is Mental Toughness Training?

Mental toughness training is another term for sports psychology. Sports psychology means taking ideas from the world of psychology and applying them to improving people's performance in sports. Psychology is the study of the mind—especially how the mind influences behavior. This book includes psychological skills and theories from the areas of mindfulness, acceptance and commitment therapy and motivation interviewing. You will also get to practice a few yoga poses. Yoga can act as a connection between the mind and the body. It is a unique way to help you solidify the concepts you are going to be learning about. Plus, yoga is lots of fun!

We talk a lot in this book about *performance*. Performance means all you do in roller derby. It's blocking, jamming, pivoting, being confident, having great character, being a great teammate—all of it! Performance refers to doing what you do with excellence.

Mental toughness training should be incorporated into your physical training. An athlete's performance is about 40% physical and 60% psychological. Some experts say mental toughness skills factor in even more! This book attempts to go beyond isolated mental toughness training to help you to truly link the psychological and physical worlds. This will allow you to have the ultimate derby experience.

> "Derby is important to me because it's the one thing I feel that I am good at. I feel the most confidence on my skates."
>
> —Annihilate-Her
>
> Age 18, Skating 4 years

Overview

This book is written to the adolescent junior roller derby participant, however it can be beneficial to skaters of all ages. Chapter 2 will help you to set your roller derby goals. Goals give you something to work towards and a way to measure your success. Chapters 3 through 9 will teach you a method of improving your mental toughness based on Gardner and Moore's Mindfulness-Acceptance-Commitment (MAC) approach to elite performance enhancement. Chapter 10 will help you to build your confidence so you can put all of the concepts from this book into action. Chapters 11 and 12 are both about teambuilding. This topic gets two chapters because derby is a team sport and the stronger your relationship is with the others on your team, the stronger your team will be! Finally, at the very end of the book is a section for your parents.

If you read my book for adults, *The Ultimate Mental Toughness Guide: Roller Derby*, you will notice that the approach in this book is very different. That book was based on traditional methods of improving mental toughness. This book includes some traditional elements such as goal setting, but most of it is a different take on mental toughness training. One difference is that while the concept of mindfulness was included in the book for adults, in this book it is a critical element of the approach. The biggest difference between the two books is the book

> "I need to keep my cool in a game and not get kicked out for things that are too aggressive so I can stay in."
>
> —Irene Yonek
>
> Age 14, Skating 5 years

for adults taught skaters to try to change their thoughts in order to feel and do better. In this book you will learn to *accept* your thoughts and feelings and be able to do well *regardless* of how you are thinking and feeling. If you are looking for a non-traditional approach to mental toughness, read on!

At the end of each chapter there is space for you to complete a short summary of what you learned about yourself and your performance. Try to be as honest as possible. Consider sharing what you write with someone else. Not only can this help another person to learn and grow, but it will reinforce the concepts for you.

It is recommended that you take a few days to a week in between reading Chapters 3 through 9. Each of those chapters has specific skills to learn and exercises that you need to complete before moving on to the next chapter. The ideas and lessons will build on each other from chapter to chapter. It's really important to feel like you understand and have mastered the concepts and skills before advancing, so repeat a chapter and its activities and exercises if needed. This is a time when it is not as important to go fast as it is to go well.

Eric Lyons Photography

Yoga

By practicing yoga, we gain control of the mind which means we gain control of our thoughts, feelings and actions as well. Through yoga, a skater achieves a willingness to be at peace with themselves and the world—becoming poised and confident. When we learn concepts through our bodies, we experience them completely and wholly. Yoga helps us to bridge the gap between learning about mental toughness skills and being mentally tough.

Our breath is all-important in the practice of yoga. The breath helps creates a connection between our minds and our bodies and can allow us to co-exist with physical and emotional discomfort. It is necessary to clarify that there is a difference between physical and/or emotional discomfort and pain. Physical discomfort means your body is getting stronger. Physical pain means a potential injury. Emotional discomfort means you are outside of your comfort zone. Emotional pain means your heart and mind are being injured, such as in the case of bullying. While becoming mentally tough means being able to deal with some discomfort, you should never try to deal with physical or emotional pain on your own—always seek help from an adult.

Yoga has been shown to do all sorts of fantastic things for us. Beyond the physical benefits of improved balance, strength and agility, practicing yoga can reduce fears, help us to feel more emotionally balanced, decrease injuries, and increase focus! Yoga is pretty much the perfect pairing for roller derby!

A little about how to breathe while practicing yoga:

Be aware of your breath. Pay attention to how you are breathing.

Breathe through your nose. Breathe in and out (inhale and exhale) through your nose.

Slow the breath. Breathe in a slow, easy and natural way.

Move with your breath. In yoga we coordinate our movements and our breath. A simple way to practice this concept is to raise and lower your arms. Breathe in when you raise your arms and breathe out when you lower your arms. Try to time your arm movements so they go along with a natural, easy breathing cycle. Expansive, lengthening movements are done on an inhale and strengthening movements are done on an exhale. When we are holding poses we continue to breathe slowly, easily and naturally, in and out through our nose. Don't hold your breath!

A few alignment principals to keep in mind while practicing yoga:

Hands. When your hands are holding your weight, spread your fingers wide and press evenly through your fingertips and the four corners of your hand.

Feet. When you are standing on your feet, spread your toes and press evenly through the four corners of each foot.

Knees. When in poses where your knee is bent, be sure the knee is positioned right over the ankle.

Yoga For Starting An Adventure

Each chapter in this book includes a yoga pose to help you experience mental toughness concepts. Now you get to practice your first yoga pose.

Star Pose. Stars have been a source of mystery and wonder ever since people first looked up at them. Stars provide direction and inspiration. Stars are strong, creating their own gravitational force. Our own sun is a star and gives us warmth and light.

This pose develops a sense of center, balance and personal power. From standing, take your feet wide apart and point your toes straight ahead. Take your arms out to the side and parallel to the floor. Activate (firm) your muscles and extend out through arms, legs and head. Spread fingers like the rays of the sum. Hold for three to five breaths.

While in the pose ask yourself the following questions:

1. What guides me?

2. How do I shine like a star?

3. Can I shine on my own and also be part of a galaxy?

Mental Toughness Quiz

Congratulations on deciding to embark on a journey to mental toughness. The skills that you learn will help you in all aspects of your life, not just roller derby. Mental toughness will help you be accomplished in school, do well on the job and be more successful in your relationships. Before you start reading the next chapter, take note of where your mental toughness skills are today by taking this Mental Toughness Quiz. Read the following statements and rate where you are according to the following scale. At the end of the book you will be asked the same questions so you can see how much you have learned and grown.

1	2	3	4	5
Not at all	A little bit	Somewhat	Mostly	Definitely!

____ I know what mental toughness is.

____ I know why I play roller derby.

____ My roller derby goals are clear.

____I am aware of my thoughts, feelings and actions.

____ I am in the present moment when I perform.

____ I notice when my focus is not where it needs to be.

____ I am able to shift my attention to where it needs to be to perform my best.

____ I accept that I will sometimes have negative thoughts and feelings on the way to achieving my derby goals.

_____ I can choose how I respond to my thoughts and feelings.

_____ My actions are in line with my values (what is important to me).

_____ I am committed to doing what it takes to perform at my best.

_____ I confident.

_____ I am a great teammate.

Scoring:

1-19 You are just starting on your mental toughness journey.

20-49 You have some mental toughness skills.

50-65 You are mentally tough!

If your score was lower that is a fantastic thing because it means you have lots of room for growth. This book will be really interesting to you because a lot of the concepts will be new. If your score was in the middle range, you have already learned some mental toughness skills along your way. This book can help you build on what you already know and add some new tricks to your mental toughness toolkit. If you scored on the higher end, you are coming into this with some advanced mental toughness skills. This book can help you if you've plateaued, met with an unexpected bump in the road or to review or enhance your skill set. For all of you, read on and remember to enjoy the ride.

You are starting on a journey towards mental toughness—
to be the best skater and person you can be!

Lydia Brewer Photography

2 GOAL SETTING

The very first step to undertaking any journey is to decide where it is you want to go. Solid roller derby goals give a purpose to our actions and a direction to head towards. Goals allow us to know when we are on track and when we have strayed down a different path. In this chapter you will get to create your own roller derby goal. Your roller derby goal is what you want to achieve in this sport. Roller derby goals don't have to be just about skating. You can create a goal around things like listening to the coach better, being kinder to teammates or eating healthier.

> "Not foul out for once."
>
> —The Crusher
>
> Age 16, Skating 6 years

Establishing an achievable, meaningful roller derby goal involves not only knowing what we want to accomplish but also understanding the following things about yourself:

- Why do you want to achieve this goal? By linking our goal to what is truly important to us it will increase our motivation and commitment.

- What do you need to be able achieve this goal? Having the resources you need to be successful you will increase your confidence that you can achieve your goal.

- What might get in the way of you achieving this goal? Knowing what might stop you from achieving your goal can help you make a plan of attack for dealing with potential barriers.

- What strengths do you have that will help you achieve this goal? By applying your inner resources such as intelligence, creativity and determination you will increase your chances of success!

Goal Mapping Aka Dream Big!

Brian Mayne created a system that uses words and pictures to communicate to both the left and right sides of the brain to help people set and achieve their goals. Try this fun way to turn your dreams into a reality by following his seven steps below.

Step 1: Dream

Imagine that you have your own magical genie just waiting to help you achieve whatever you really want. Whatever you think about becomes a wish and commands your genie. Close your eyes for a little while and imagine what your ideal roller derby life would be like. Think a big dream full of heartfelt wishes. When you open your eyes immediately start writing out a list on the following page of everything you want to achieve.

Cory Lund Photography

My Wishes

1.

2.

3.

4.

5.

6.

7.

8.

9.

10.

Step 2: Order

When you are dreaming of the way you would like your roller derby life to be, what stands out as the main goal? Achieving this goal might even help you to attain your other goals. Choose the one thing from your list that you feel most excited about and write it on the left-brain goal mapping template (page 14) in the center box marked 'main-goal.' Write it as if you've already achieved it. Such as, "I am skating in three jams in a row." Now choose four more wishes from your list and write them in the same way, this time in the boxes marked "sub-goals' on either side of your main goal.

Step 3: Draw

On the right-brain goal mapping template (page 15), draw pictures of your goals. Your drawings can be as simple or fancy as you choose only use lots of color as this really makes your genie take notice. Start by drawing a picture of your main-goal in the center circle and then pictures of your sub-goals on the four branches on either side.

Step 4: Why

Think now about why you want your goals. What are your strongest reasons and what good feelings does the thought of achieving your goals give you, such as happiness, love and family? Write your reasons in the top boxes of your left-brain template and then draw pictures of your reasons on your right-brain template.

Step 5: When

Now choose a date for when you want to achieve your goals. You may want your goals straight away but all genies need a little time to work their magic. What do you think will be a good timeline for you and your genie to achieve your goals? Write the date or how old you will be on both maps in the small circle and box just below your main goal. Now write today's date in the circle and box at the bottom of the page.

Step 6: How

Next think of some of the things you can do that will help you move towards your goal, such as learning new skills. Once you have thought of some actions you can take write them in the boxes marked HOW on your left-brain goal template, then draw the pictures on your right-brain goal template. Put the action you can start on first on the bottom branch of the trunk with the other actions moving up towards the top.

Step 7: Who

The last step is to decide who you would like to help you. Most goals will normally need some sort of help from someone. It could be a member of your family, your coach or a teammate who you would like to help. Write the person's name in the box marked WHO on your left-brain goal map opposite the action you want help with. Then draw pictures on your right-brain goal map.

Finally, sign your goal map and say your goals every morning while looking at the pictures and imagine how it will feel to achieve your greatest dreams.

Left-brain Goal Mapping template for words

Right-brain Goal Mapping template for pictures

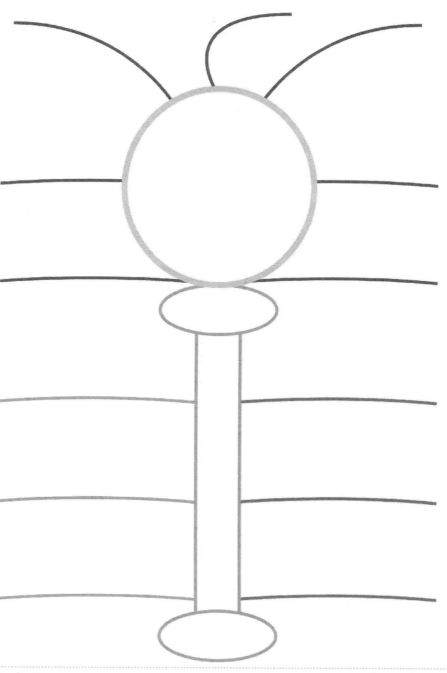

S.M.A.R.T. Goals

Goals need to be clear in order for us to note our progress towards them. The acronym S.M.A.R.T. can remind us of all the essential ingredients of a great goal. S.M.A.R.T. stands for specific, measurable, action-oriented, realistic and time-limited.

Specific. Goals should be clear, rather than vague or general. Instead of saying, "I want to be a stronger jammer" try "I want to be able to get through the pack on my own, without assistance."

Measurable. There should be a way to measure your progress towards your goal or a way to know when you've achieved it. Including elements that can be measured in numbers can help, such as number of penalties, number of laps, number of points, number of assists, etc.

Action-oriented. Your goal should be about things you want to do, not things you don't want to do. Use the "rock rule." If a rock can do it, it isn't a good goal. For example, the goal "I'm not going to swear today" is not the greatest goal because a rock can do that. Try making the goal into something that requires you to take action. For example, "I will say 'thank you' when someone helps me." What are the action steps that you need to take to be able to get to your goal?

Realistic. You goal should be something you are both willing and able to do. Goals should be difficult enough to challenge you, but realistic enough to be achievable. Based on how far you've come and where you're at now, where do you think you can go? A big goal can be broken down into bite-size, easily digestible pieces that will help you to stair-step your way to success. You can place these steps in the "HOW" section of the goal mapping templates.

> "My biggest goal is to just continue to be in derby for like a long time. I want to continue to do it just as long as I possibly can. I have bad knees now and I'm only 15 so I hope they don't give out."
>
> —Kick N Ash
>
> Age 15, Skating 6 years

Time-limited. There needs to be a deadline to when you will accomplish your goal. Time frames tied to your goal give you a sense of urgency and help to motivate you. A good guideline is to set goals that you can achieve within 3 to 6 months.

Example of a S.M.A.R.T. goal:

What do you want to achieve?

I will be able to skate in 3 back-to-back jams during a game by three months from now. I want to be equally as strong on the third jam as the first one.

Why do you want to achieve this?

Being at the top is very important to me. It shows the world I know how to work hard and push myself.

What do you need to be able to achieve this goal?

I need to have improved strength and endurance.

What might get in the way of you achieving this goal?

An injury, inconsistent attendance at practice, giving up because it's too hard.

What strengths or resources do you have that will help you achieve this goal?

My coaches support me in this goal. I am already one of the stronger jammers on my team.

Just as important as setting a goal is reviewing it regularly. After one month go back and look over your goal, evaluating it. Check on your progress towards you goal. Maybe you've already achieved it and it's time to set a new one? Maybe you haven't made any progress towards it at all? If that is the case, see how the goal needs to be adjusted. It may be that the goal was set too far away from where you are today. It may be that the goal is not broken down into the correct action steps. It may mean you need more support or resources to make it happen. Re-evaluate your goals monthly—**S**pecific, **M**easurable, **A**ction-oriented, **R**ealistic, **T**imely, **E**valuate and **R**e-evaluate. With these added steps you have made your goal even S.M.A.R.T.E.R.!

Now you can take a look at your Main Goal from the goal mapping exercise and make sure it is a SMART goal using the My S.M.A.R.T. Goal Worksheet on the next page. Does your goal have all the SMART ingredients? If not, make changes as needed.

> "I want to be able to get through some of the biggest girls. I let them hit me out because I think oh gosh she's bigger than me."
>
> —Ally Oops
>
> Age 17, Skating 4 years

My S.M.A.R.T. Goal Worksheet

What do you want to achieve (This is your main roller derby goal)?

_____

_____

Check to make sure your goal is S.M.A.R.T.:

__Is it specific?

__Is it measurable?

__Is it action-oriented?

__Is it realistic?

__Is it time-limited?

Make your goal even S.M.A.R.T.E.R. by Evaluating and Re-Evaluating it monthly!

It takes 21 days to establish a new behavior.

Stages Of Change

In the early 1980s, James Prochaska and Carlo DiClemente created a model to explain the process of change. Setting out to achieve a big goal is setting out to make a big change from where you're at right now. Knowing that there are stages people go through when undertaking a big change can be helpful in understanding where you're at in this process and how to move yourself forward. There are five stages of change—precontemplation, contemplation, preparation, action and maintenance.

Precontemplation (not ready): If you are in this stage, you are not ready to do anything differently than you are doing now. You may not be ready because you don't believe you can do it or have had bad experiences trying to achieve goals in the past. Even if your teammates, family or coaches are pushing you to do something it won't make a difference. In fact, if you are in this stage and are being pushed to achieve something, you may appear rebellious. A skater in this stage may be thinking, *I can't improve my endurance* or *I don't want to improve my endurance.*

Contemplation: If you are in this stage you are thinking about the possibility of achieving your goals. You may be on the fence about it. A skater in this stage may be thinking, *I would like to have better endurance but I'm not sure I want to put the work into it.*

> "I want to be an A level jammer. They're able to get through easily and score a whole bunch of points. I have trouble getting through the pack if I don't have an assist and it honestly terrifies me."
>
> —Blackheart Blockher
>
> Age 14, Skating 4 years

Preparation: In this stage of change you are ready to take action and are starting to take small steps. You will be planning how you will accomplish your goal. This could include determining who will need to be involved, looking at financial costs or researching information. In this stage you will be breaking down your goal into the small, bite-size steps needed to make it happen. A skater in this stage may be thinking, *I am going to start running outside of practice to improve my endurance.*

Action: This stage of change is all about taking action. You know what needs to be done and you are committed to doing it. A skater in this stage may say, *I have started running outside of practice twice a week to have better endurance during games.*

Maintenance: In this stage you don't have any desire to return to your previous levels of performing. Taking the steps needed to achieve your goals has become a regular part of who you are. You are on an upward climb and intend to keep it going. A skater in this stage may say, *I have been running twice a week for a while now and I like the improvement I see in my endurance during games.*

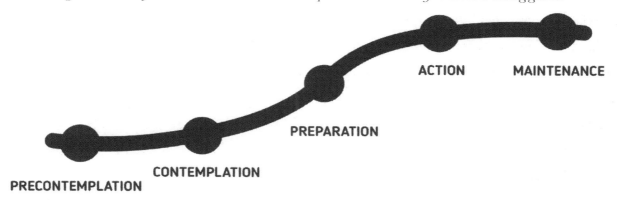

ACTION   **MAINTENANCE**

PREPARATION

CONTEMPLATION

PRECONTEMPLATION

Maximizing Commitment

The words we use when we talk about our goals can give us clues as to how ready to commit to them we actually are. There are four types of "talk" we use when talking about making changes—resistance talk, stuck talk, change talk, and commitment talk. When we are resistant to working towards our goals we may make excuses or blame circumstances or others outside of ourselves for not being where we want to be.

"I want to be able to do better apexes for sure. I can do them forwards but I want to be able to do them backwards and land backwards. I always get hit and die usually."

—Lucky Harms

Age 13, Skating 4 years

Examples of resistance talk are:

The coach hates me

My gear sucks

They won't let me have a chance

When we are stuck and not moving towards our goals we may use words that show how dedicated to staying the same we are:

I just don't get along with other females

I'm as fast as I can be

I will never hit as hard as her

When we are starting to move towards making the commitment to achieve our goals we use change talk. Change talk includes the word 'I', rather than 'you,' because it indicates we are starting to look inward to what we can do, rather than outward at all the reasons we can't do it. Your change talk communicates a desire to achieve your goals, recognizes your ability to achieve your goals, and acknowledges a reason to achieve your goals. As you move from being *motivated* to achieve your goals to being *committed* to achieving your goals, your words will start to reflect that you are taking action, rather than just thinking about it.

Using words like these show a lower level of commitment:

I hope to…

I plan to…

I will try to…

Using words like these shows a higher level of commitment:

I will…

I am going to…

I promise to…

If you are not sure about committing to your goals, asking yourself questions like the following can help:

- Suppose you don't work towards _____(your goal), what do you think your life will be like one year from now?

- If you were completely successful in achieving_____(your goal), how would things be different for you?

- On a scale from 1 to 10, how important is it for you to_____(your goal)? What would need to happen to increase that number?

When we have committed to our goals, our talk will be action-oriented and in the present tense because we are actually doing it!

Whatever you feed is going to grow. If you put your energy into talking about how you can't do something or don't want to do something, then *not* changing is going to gain power. If you talk about what you can do or are willing to do or even better yet, *are* doing, those words will move you in the direction you want to go.

| I can't/ I don't want to. | I might be able. to do it. | This is how to do it. | I'm doing it. | I did it! |

Words are powerful.

Tipping The Scale In Favor Of Commitment

"I would like to get less penalties and communicate things quicker sounding less frantic. I sound kind of bossy. Three penalties would be my main number. I would like to have less than three."

—Ginger Slap

Age 15, Skating 4 years

Working towards your goals can be a lot of work and is a big commitment. One way to maximize your motivation for commitment is to weigh the pros and cons. Complete the Decisional Balance Scale Worksheet for a goal that you have been unsure or ambivalent about committing to. On one side of the scale write all the reasons to change or accomplish your goal. On the other side of the scale write all the reasons not to change or accomplish your goal. It is up to you to decide what it will take to tip the scale in favor of commitment!

Lydia Brewer Photography

Reasons To Change   Reasons To Stay The Same

Decisional Balance Scale Worksheet

Yoga For Strength

Warrior II Pose. Warriors are courageous, honorable, disciplined and are committed to what is important to them. They are humble and compassionate. Warriors have inner and outer strength and a definite sense of purpose.

Embody the qualities of a warrior with this pose which can make you feel super strong, steady and confident. Stand with legs wide apart. Turn your left foot so that it is perpendicular to your right foot (the left heel should line up with the inner part of the right foot). Breathe in and lift arms up parallel to the floor with palms facing down. Exhale and bend the left knee until it is right over the ankle. Keep your torso settled in the center and not leaning to the front or back. Press your feet firmly into the ground and feel strength flowing up through your body. Hold for three to five breaths.

As you hold this pose, think about your back hand representing your past and your front hand representing your future. We want to be aware of the past and how it has effected us and also aware of our future goals, with our eyes looking ahead. We don't want to be stuck in the past or too worried about the future. We keep our weight balanced in the middle—in the present.

As you work in this pose, reflect on the following questions:

1. Who supports me?

2. Can I be fierce and also in control?

3. How am I strong like a warrior?

"I want to be on Team USA. I want as a team to be ranked number one. I think if we really try we can make it by the time I'm 18. I want to be able to make a 360 jump. I can do one really slow but I want to be able to eat breathe and sleep 360. I want to be able to do 8 second laps. I get like 9 now but I get slower, it's not consistent. I want to be able to pace myself. I want solid muscles. Like Suzie Hotrod. Have you seen her? "

—Slim Reaper

Age 16, Skating 7 years

You have set your goals and know where it is you want to go.

What I Have Learned About Myself And My Roller Derby Performance

In each chapter of this book, you are likely to learn a variety of new things about yourself and your derby performance. After you read each chapter, complete this form as soon as possible. The purpose of this is to ensure that you are learning and remembering the important concepts from each chapter.

1._____

_____

_____

2._____

_____

_____

3._____

_____

_____

4._____

_____

_____

5._____

_____

_____

3 THE MAC APPROACH

MAC is an approach which seeks to enhance your mental toughness through improved attention and poise. *Attention* in sports psychology is the ability to focus on the important things as needed. *Poise* is using actions which will help you accomplish your goals and stay true to your values even if you are having negative thoughts and feelings. You will be able to do this by learning new ideas, learning and practicing new skills, and completing other cool activities.

The M in MAC stands for Mindfulness.

The A in MAC stands for Acceptance.

The C in MAC stands for Commitment.

Mindfulness training will allow you to grow your ability to be self-aware. Self-awareness means being able to notice what you are thinking and feeling. You will be able to experience these thoughts and feelings without judging them as being good or bad. Self-awareness also allows us to know what we are focusing on at any one moment. That way we can shift our attention where it is needed for the task at hand. Your mindfulness skills will also enhance your ability to be in the present moment.

Acceptance is understanding that there will be obstacles, challenges, and unexpected events along the road of your roller derby career. These obstacles, challenges and unexpected events may make you feel bad, upset or uncomfortable. Acceptance means you acknowledge this and don't try to fight it or want it not to be so. It just is.

Commitment means you are taking the steps needed to achieve your roller derby goals. Commitment is different from motivation. Motivation is having the desire for something. Commitment is actually taking the steps needed to get that something. Motivation is nice. Commitment is necessary.

MAC is different from traditional mental toughness approaches, or Psychological Skills Training (PST) approaches, because those teach the athlete to try to think and feel better. With a PST approach, there is

> "When I get angry I just hit somebody. I just wreck people. It's not really what we need at that moment. I'm just hitting someone to hit someone. My team might need me to be somewhere else."
>
> —Ally Oops
>
> Age 17, Skating 4 years

an attempt to control or avoid thoughts and feelings considered to be negative or bad. Say you are feeling nervous before a big game. Using a traditional PST approach, you would tell yourself things intended to make you feel more confident such as, "You've got this!" What is exciting about the MAC approach is you will be able to perform well *and* have negative thoughts and feelings.

Face it, how successful have you been at completely getting rid of the thoughts and feelings that you consider to be bad? To add to this difficulty, sometimes trying to change the thoughts and feelings can make them even worse, because you could be constantly scanning your brain to see if any bad thoughts or feelings are lurking. This means you are putting even more focus on the bad thoughts or feelings— intensifying them.

Understand the difference between motivation and commitment. Motivation is having the desire for something. Commitment is taking the steps necessary to achieve it. Motivation is nice, but commitment is necessary.

27

Thoughts, Feelings And Actions

Let's take a minute and talk about what thoughts, feelings and actions are. *Thoughts* are the beliefs, attitudes, perceptions and ideas we have in our heads. *Feelings* are the emotions and sensations we have in our bodies and hearts. *Actions* are the things we say and do. If we allow them to, our thoughts can lead to us feeling a certain way and that can lead us to doing or saying certain things.

Here are some examples of feelings related to roller derby performance:

Sad	Excited
Angry	Frustrated
Scared	Worried

Here are some examples of thoughts related to roller derby performance:

I don't think I can do that	*This is easy*
My coach doesn't think I'm working hard	*I hate this*
I don't want to let my family down	*That was so fun!*

Here are some examples of actions related to roller derby performance:

Smiling	Listening
Giving a compliment	Saying thank you
Rolling your eyes	Walking out during practice

We also experience feelings in our bodies which are called *physiological responses*. These automatic responses can come from being under stress and can make us think we are in danger when we aren't.

Here are some examples of physiological responses related to roller derby performance:

Queasy stomach	Rapid breathing
Sweaty palms	Butterflies
Increased heartrate	Tense muscles

What are some feelings you consider to be negative or bad?

What are some thoughts you consider to be negative or bad?

What are some physiological responses you consider to be negative or bad?

What are some feelings you consider to be positive or good?

What are some thoughts you consider to be positive or good?

What are some physiological responses you consider to be positive or good?

A wide range of emotions and bodily sensations are a natural part of being human. They make our life rich. Can you imagine what life would be like if you only felt the "good" emotions? How would you even know they were the good ones if you didn't have something to compare them to? Would you be able to appreciate the good times if that was all you ever had?

> "My own emotions are what get in the way. I get in my head and I start to mentally shut myself down and it makes it worse, I don't let anything out, I bottle it up."
>
> —Annihilate-Her
>
> Age 18, Skating 4 years

A wide range of emotions are a natural part of being human.

Negative thoughts and feelings can negatively affect our performance because we are focusing on them and not on what we should be focusing on. We are overly focused on ourselves and what is going on in our head when we should be focusing on some other important aspect of our performance. We are allowing our thoughts and feelings to distract us from the task at hand. Can you think of some times when you got stuck in your head and it negatively affected your performance?

> "When I come to practice sometimes I'm goofing around and not committing 100% to it. I don't really think about my goals so maybe I should start doing that."
>
> —Tap Out
>
> Age 13, Skating 3 ½ years

Trying to avoid certain thoughts and feelings can also negatively affect our performance because we are not acting in ways that will get us to our goals. In those moments, escaping from feeling bad or uncomfortable is what is driving our actions. For example, if you know the coach ended up making you feel bad at the last practice, you may skip the next one because you don't want that to happen again. Skipping practice is not going to help you to achieve your roller derby goals. That is an obvious example of avoiding feeling bad. There are subtle ways we do this too such as choosing a partner for a drill because they are not as skilled as we are. This will allow us to evade those yucky thoughts and feelings like self-doubt, worry, frustration, and jealousy. Can you think of some times when you were trying to make yourself feel better and that ended up taking you further away from your goals rather than closer to them? The existence of certain thoughts and feelings is not the problem, it is our attempts to change, control, or avoid them that interferes with us being our best. It can be freeing to know you don't have to be change, control, or avoid negative thoughts and feelings.

Complete The Performance Rating Form

Next complete the Performance Rating Form. First list the performance barriers that have got in the way of you doing your best in the last two weeks. Then look at each of the performance areas and rate them from 0 to10 according to how satisfied you are with your performance in each area and how much of an impact your performance barriers had on you doing your best. Areas with low satisfaction should have high impact of barriers and vice versa.

Photo by Keli Burch-Moran

Performance Rating Form

Please list all of the things that have got in the way of your performance (performance barriers) in the last 2 weeks (such as negative thoughts, negative emotions, problems with teammates and lack of concentration):

1. _____

2. _____

3. _____

4. _____

5. _____

0	1	2	3	4	5	6	7	8	9	10
None		Mild			Moderate		Strong		Extreme	

Please rate each of the following using the 0 to 10 scale above:

Performance Area	Rate your satisfaction with your performance in each area (0 to 10)	How much do your performance barriers impact each area (0 to 10)
Practice/Training		
Games/Competitions		
Relationships With Coaches		
Relationships with Teammates		
Other (Please describe)		

Get your head out of your skate's way!

Being In The Zone

You may have heard athletes talk about being "in the zone" during a particularly successful game or moment during a game. If you have ever felt this experience, those were most likely the times when you played your absolute best. When you are in the zone:

- You're completely involved in what you are doing.

- You have a feeling of being outside everyday reality.

- There is a clear understanding of what you want to achieve.

- You aren't aware of being tired or sore.

- You know that you can do the task at hand.

- There is a sense of timelessness.

- You're not worried about yourself.

- There is a balance between your skill level and the challenge.

- You're not thinking about what your body is doing.

- Your actions feel effortless.

"It just happens really fast—jamming when your wall makes a hole for you and you slide through. Empty minded—when I hit the wall I wasn't even worried about it."

—Tap Out

Age 13, Skating 3 ½ years

According to positive psychologist, Mihaly Csikszentmihalyi, in this state "Your whole being is involved, and you're using your skills to the utmost." This book teaches you how to maximize your chances of experiencing zone-like performance by being:

Mindful

Self-aware

Focused on what is relevant

In the moment

Confident

It will be important for you to practice the new mental toughness skills you are learning just like you practice the physical elements of roller derby. Your performance will advance because you will learn to practice and compete more efficiently and consistently and you will develop improved attention and poise.

> "Not really having to think about things, it just happens and I'm not afraid to mess up. I'm confident in the skills I have."
>
> —Brozilla
>
> Age 16, Skating 2 ½ years

Breath Counting Exercise

Now you're going to complete your first mindfulness exercise. This exercise will help you to learn self-awareness, be in the present moment and to begin to create distance between your actions and your thoughts and feelings. Spend at least a few minutes with this exercise.

Take a comfortable seat and pay attention to your breath. Breathe naturally. Breathe in and allow the breath to fully enter your body until your lower belly expands. Then breathing out, softly allow the breath to ease out through your nose. Your belly should rise and fall naturally with each breath. Let the breath fill your lower belly as if it were a balloon. As you relax into the breath, you can begin silently counting each full cycle of breath, noting "one" on the first exhale, "two" on the next exhale, and so on up to "ten." When you reach "ten," begin again with "one." If you realize that you have stopped counting and are caught up in thinking, simply take another breath and go back to "one."

While you are sitting, you may realize that you are thinking about something else besides your breath and counting. At that moment, take a deep breath and recognize that. In that moment of realization, you have come back to the present moment. It is said that as soon as you become aware of a thought, it will disappear! When we are thinking of a thing, we are lost in it, lost in thinking about whatever it is. But when we become aware of our

> "Honestly all that's going through my head when I'm in it is 'jammer jammer jammer.'"
>
> —Kick N Ash
>
> Age 15, skating 6 years

33

thinking, then we are in a secondary state, becoming observers of our thoughts. The actual thinking of the thing is gone, and there is either just awareness or we begin a new thought based on that awareness. Either way, the original thinking has vanished.

Basic Centering Exercise

This mindfulness exercise teaches you to be able to focus on the present moment and to be able to shift your attention between your breath, your environment, your body and your thoughts. Eventually, you will be able to complete this and the other mindfulness exercises in this book by memory.

Find a comfortable sitting position. Notice the position of your feet, arms and hands. Allow your eyes to close gently. Breathe in and out gently and deeply several times. Notice the sound and feel of your own breath as you breathe in and out.

Now focus your attention on your surroundings. Notice any sounds that may be occurring. What sounds do you hear inside the room? What sounds do you hear outside the room? Now focus your attention on the areas where your body touches the chair. What does it feel like? Now notice the spot where your feet are touching the floor. Now notice anything you may be feeling in the rest of your body and notice how those sensations may change over time without any effort on your part. Don't try to alter these sensations, just notice them as they occur.

Now let your focus go to your thoughts. See if you can notice any doubts or other thoughts without doing anything but noticing them. Just notice your worries or concerns or any other thoughts as though they are elements of a parade passing through your mind. Don't try to make them go away or change them in any way. Now allow yourself to focus on what you want your derby life to be about. What is most important to you? What do you want to do with your skills?

Remain comfortable for a few more moments and slowly let yourself focus once again on any sounds and movements occurring around you. Once again notice your own breathing. When you are ready, open your eyes and notice that you feel focused and attentive.

Yoga For Seeing Things From A Different Angle

Triangle Pose. A triangle is very strong, which is why you will see its shape used in the building of bridges or other structures. A triangle has three sides which is the minimum you need to make a shape (or else it's just a line) or support something (think of a 3-legged chair, camera tripod or a tricycle).

Stand with your legs wide apart. Turn your left foot to face forward—your left heel will be aiming towards the inside of your right foot. Lift your arms up parallel to the floor. Reach your left arm forward and stretch your left hand down to your shin, ankle or floor depending on how flexible you are. Keep both of your legs straight. Stretch your right arm towards the sky. Repeat on the other side.

As you work with this pose be aware of what is happening within your body and your mind. As you hold this pose think about the following:

1. What are three of my strengths?
2. When do I become unstable?
3. How do my thoughts, feelings and actions interact?

In-Between Chapters Mindfulness Exercises:

Please take a few days to a week before you start the next chapter to practice the skills you learned in this chapter.

1. Breath Counting Exercise: practice this daily
2. Basic Centering Exercise: practice this every other day.

You are ready to become stronger and more flexible, inside and out!

Cory Lund Photography

What I Have Learned About Myself And My Roller Derby Performance

In each chapter of this book, you are likely to learn a variety of new things about yourself and your derby performance. After you read each chapter, complete this form as soon as possible. The purpose of this is to ensure that you are learning and remembering the important concepts from each chapter.

1._____

_____

_____

2._____

_____

_____

3._____

_____

_____

4._____

_____

_____

5._____

_____

_____

4 MINDFULNESS AND THE MIND

By now you have practiced your first mindfulness activities, the Breath Counting Exercise and the Basic Centering Exercise, several times and should be getting really good at them. Being mindful is the opposite of being mindless. Think about something you do without fully pay attention to what you are doing. Walking between classes? Doing the dishes? Listen to a teacher's lecture? We can complete many activities mindlessly because we have done them a million times or we don't really care that much about them.

Now think of an activity that requires you to fully pay attention to be able to do it. Doing a headstand? Walking across a balance beam? Completing a difficult math problem? We must be mindful to complete these activities because they require all of our concentration either because they are difficult for us or very important to us. Being mindful is the opposite of being mindless. When we are mindful we are fully absorbed in our activities with 100% of our bodies and our minds. We do this purposefully. If you have ever tried to do something challenging without approaching it mindfully you probably didn't feel you did the best you could do. Mindfulness will improve your derby performance by allowing you to:

- Increase your self-awareness

- Enjoy the full roller derby experience

- Tolerate upsetting thoughts, feelings and body sensations

- Create distance between your thoughts and feelings and your actions

- Control where your attention is focused

- Be in the present moment

The mindfulness skill of self-awareness will allow you to be able to notice your thoughts, feelings and actions. You will be able to notice them as simply *being* without judging them as being good or bad. By becoming an observer of our internal world, distance is created between what we are experiencing inside and our actions. This gives us time to determine what our actions will be. Mindfulness will also allow you to be aware of what you are paying attention to at any one time. When we are aware of what we are focusing on, it makes it possible to know if we need to shift our attention to something more helpful to our performance. Last, mindfulness skills increase our ability to be fully present in the immediate moment. Being present enhances your performance because you are putting 100% into experiencing this fantastic moment without distraction.

> "I need to not hold grudges. Because when people bring stuff up in practice saying I'm doing something wrong it gets on my nerves. But to be honest we're all not the best at something."
>
> -Irene Yonek
>
> Age 14, Skating 5 years

The mindfulness exercises in this book will help you to be able to develop the skills needed to do all of these things. You will need to practice them daily while you are reading this book and beyond. Building mindfulness and other mental toughness skills take training just like building physical skills takes training. You can think of mindfulness exercises as pushups for your mind.

A Mindful Minute Exercise

This exercise will allow you to notice your thoughts without needing to respond to them or judge them as being good or bad. Find a quiet place and sit comfortably. Eliminate distractions such as TV or music. Close your eyes and for one minute simply notice your thoughts. Allow them to wander but pay attention to where they go. Don't try to change your thoughts or judge them. Notice how your thoughts come and go. You don't have to take any action to make this happen. Notice how one thought leads to another without you having to do anything at all. No single thought lingers for long. If an upsetting thought passes through your mind simply observe the thought, note it, and then let it pass gently by as if it is attached to a balloon.

After one minute, think about what that experience was like for you? Think about the thoughts that went through your mind. One lesson to take away from this exercise is the knowledge that our thoughts are not always absolute realities and our thoughts do not always require immediate action.

Automatic Behaviors

Automatic behaviors are the things we do without being aware of it. This happens because we have developed patterns in how we react to certain thoughts and feelings. Over time these responses become automatic which means we do them without thinking. This can become a problem when our automatic behaviors aren't in our best interest. Many times we develop these kinds of patterns in response to negative or upsetting emotions. The emotions don't feel good so we react in an attempt to avoid feeling that way. These tactics can help us to feel good in the short run but don't help us to achieve our roller derby goals.

"I experience pure joy. I feel the best when I am skating my best. I feel like I am unstoppable. I am happy and just ready to skate when I feel good."

—Annihilate-Her

Age 18, Skating 4 years

Self-awareness is critical as you begin to unlearn automatic behaviors that don't work and start to replace them with new behaviors that are in line with where you want to go with your roller derby career. Self-awareness will also help you to understand that emotions are experiences that don't need to be controlled or avoided—even negative ones. In due course, your enhanced self-awareness will allow you to increase the actions that you need to achieve your ultimate roller derby goals.

Sam Himelstein, founder of the Center for Adolescent Studies, came up with a great analogy that demonstrates the striking difference between automatic behaviors and mindful behaviors. Think of a how a dog acts when a person is waving a bone in front of its face. The dog will be ultra-focused on that bone and little else, turning its head this way and that way to follow the bone. Now what will happen if the person throws the bone?

The dog will more than likely chase the bone.

Now consider this same scenario with a lion. What will the lion do if a person waves a bone in front of its face and then throws it? Is the lion going to chase the bone?

It could chase the bone.

Or it could eat the person.

When the bone is being waved in front of its face, the dog sees nothing but the bone. The bone represents all of the dog's reality—it consumes the dog. The lion's mind, on the other hand, is a lot different. The lion can see past one aspect of the situation to the bigger picture and can make the most sensible decision. The lion could be thinking, "Doesn't this person know they have way more bones in their body? I could eat this person for breakfast." The bone is just a little sliver of the lion's larger reality—that gives the lion the ability to choose and have more control over itself.

Our emotions can rule us in the same way the bone controls the dog. They can overtake us and become our whole reality. With mindfulness practice you can experience your emotions as just one aspect of your larger reality. The process of being mindful will create space between you and your emotions and allow you to be able to respond in the way you want to instead of reacting automatically. Remember the lion-mind and be the king of your inner jungle.

Be the lion, not the dog.

Mindfulness Attention Awareness Scale (MAAS)

For most of you reading this book, mindfulness is a new skill you are learning. In order for you to make sure you are making progress, you are going to take a mindfulness quiz to see where your skills in this area are right now. In Chapter 9 you will take this test again and hopefully your scores will have gone up.

Mindful Attention Awareness Scale (MAAS) Day-to-Day Experiences

Instructions: Below is a collection of statements about your everyday experience. Using the 1-6 scale below, please indicate how frequently or infrequently you currently have each experience. Please answer according to what really reflects your experience rather than what you think your experience should be. Please treat each item separately from every other item.

1	2	3	4	5	6
Always	**Frequently**	**Somewhat frequently**	**Somewhat infrequently**	**Infrequently**	**Never**

I could be experiencing some emotion and not be conscious of it until sometime later.

        1   2   3   4   5   6

I break or spill things because of carelessness, not paying attention, or thinking of something else.

        1   2   3   4   5   6

I find it difficult to stay focused on what's happening in the present.

        1   2   3   4   5   6

I tend to walk quickly to get where I'm going without paying attention to what I experience along the way.

        1   2   3   4   5   6

I tend not to notice feelings of physical tension or discomfort until they really grab my attention.

        1   2   3   4   5   6

I forget a person's name almost as soon as I've been told it for the first time.

        1   2   3   4   5   6

It seems I am "running on automatic," without much awareness of what I'm doing.

I rush through activities without being really attentive to them.

1   2   3   4   5   6

I get so focused on the goal I want to achieve that I lose touch with what I'm doing right now to get there.

1   2   3   4   5   6

I do jobs or tasks automatically, without being aware of what I'm doing.

1   2   3   4   5   6

I find myself listening to someone with one ear, doing something else at the same time.

1   2   3   4   5   6

I go places on 'automatic pilot' and then wonder why I went there.

1   2   3   4   5   6

I find myself preoccupied with the future or the past.

1   2   3   4   5   6

I find myself doing things without paying attention.

1   2   3   4   5   6

I snack without being aware that I'm eating.

1   2   3   4   5   6

Scoring: To score the MAAS scale, simply compute an average of the 15 items. Higher scores reflect higher levels of mindfulness.

Mindfulness is a necessary skill to have on your road to developing mental toughness. There is not much we can change about ourselves if we are not even aware of what we are doing. Being mindful will allow you to be completely in the moment in your derby activities. You will be able to recognize when you are distracted from the task at hand and be able to refocus as needed.

Mindfulness is not clearing the mind so that it is blank, rather it is choosing what you want to focus on and then doing so with intention. Mindfulness is not a relaxation technique or a way to think positively. Using this book's approach to mental toughness, you don't need to change your thoughts and feelings to positive ones in order to be successful.

Cory Lund Photography

Cognitive Fusion

The word *fusion* means things are joined together to form one. *Cognitive* has to do with all the stuff going on in our heads such as ideas, memories, beliefs, images, and thoughts. So, cognitive fusion refers to us becoming too focused on what is going on in our heads. We make decisions based on our internal experiences rather than what is really going on around us. This can become problematic when we treat our thoughts like they are absolute truths or as if they are a command we have to obey.

Cognitive Defusion is the opposite of Cognitive Fusion. This is where we can observe our thoughts and see them for what they are.

"Since I couldn't ever get through the pack I felt like I was completely worthless to the team. I thought I'd never be good enough. When I get really angry or sad I tend to shut down and that got in the way of me improving. Since I felt like I wasn't good enough I never did my best I could at it."

—Blackheart Blockher

Age 14. Skating 4 years

Thoughts:

- May or may not be true

- Are not a command you have to obey

- Are not a threat to you

- Are not something happening in the physical realm

- Can be allowed to come and go on their own

 There is a difference between reacting to an actual event and thinking about such an event. This can be a difficult concept to grasp at first because the way humans are designed, our minds will react the same way to a real and imaginary event. This causes us to be emotionally and physically responsive to our thoughts. Try it for yourself—think about a time you blocked someone so effectively that they took a huge fall. In just remembering an event you will experience the same emotions and have the same physical reactions as if it is actually happening right now. You may feel excitement and aggression. Your muscles may tense up. Your heart rate may increase and your breathing may become more rapid. In reading this book, you are learning to be able to tell the difference between what *is* and what the mind *tells us* is. This will allow you to be able to observe your thoughts and recognize them as just being something our busy minds create.

When we can separate ourselves from our internal processes (thoughts and feelings) we can realize that they don't require us to act on them. This can be quite empowering. It means when you are angry or scared or frustrated, you don't have to let those emotions get in the way of what you really want to be doing—becoming the best roller derby skater you can be. Can you think of some examples from your own life when you were able to create distance between what your mind told you and the believability of those thoughts?

Typically, when we get angry, scared, frustrated or other upsetting feeling, there is some event that happens outside of us. Perhaps our teammate says something that makes us angry. According to Stimulus-Response Theory, this event is called the *stimulus*. After the stimulus occurs we respond with some behavior such as crying, yelling, stomping off, punching something, etc.

Stimulus   ⟶   Response

Through the process of mindfulness, you can create cognitive defusion—separation between yourself and your emotions. Viktor Frankl, an existential psychologist and holocaust survivor, said "Between stimulus and response there is a space. In that space is our power to choose our response. In that response lies our growth and our freedom."

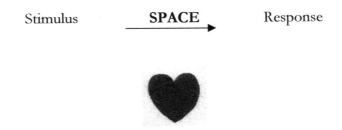

46

A Mindful Snack Exercise

You might wonder what eating a snack has to do with improving your roller derby performance. When learning a new skill, it is easier to apply it to something simple, relaxed and familiar before trying it during a complicated, stressful scenario. We will build on these mindfulness exercises, slowly making them more roller derby-relevant as we go.

Choose a quiet moment to select something to eat. Select something simple such as raisins, fruit snacks, orange slices or a cookie. First, without picking it up, just look at your food for a moment and become aware of the color, shape, and texture.

Now, pick up your food and allow other senses to come into play. While you are completing this exercise, you are likely to notice a variety of thoughts that aren't related to this task. Just notice them without judging them as good or bad, right or wrong, but simply an activity in your mind that comes and goes. The specific thoughts do not matter, just your ability to notice and focus on the feelings and sensations that this exercise creates. Allow yourself to feel the sensations in more and more detail. This will strengthen your concentration.

Holding, seeing, and touching: Examine it as if you were an alien and had never seen such a thing before. What do its features look like? How does it fit in your hand? How does it feel on the pads of your fingers?

Smelling: Hold the food to your nose and smell its aroma. Really get a sense of it. Does the smell arouse your senses? Does your mouth or stomach react?

Placing: Place the food on your tongue. Just hold it there. Examine it with your mouth, without chewing. How are you reacting? How does this food feel?

> "When you're upset you just want to skate all the upsetness out, push it out through your legs, push it out through your body."
>
> —The Crusher
>
> Age 16, Skating 6 years

Tasting: Place the food between your teeth and bite. Notice how your mouth and tongue move around in order to bite it. When you bite, notice the texture. Note the flavors as they release. Pause after a few bites and experience the flavor and texture in your mouth. Continue chewing and noticing. Does the taste change?

Swallowing: Note the position your mouth takes as it gets ready to swallow. Finally, swallow the food.

Continue to mindfully eat the rest of your snack. Notice any sounds around you or thoughts you are having as if they are words or images sitting on fluffy white clouds that are slowly floating by. Gently bring your focus back to your task at hand. Having a variety of thoughts is normal; be patient with yourself. The fact of the matter is the mind will always tend to wander. Remain in the moment with your eating and you will increase your ability to pay attention.

A Mindful Chore Exercise

This mindfulness exercise requires you to do a chore that most find boring, tedious or awful—washing a dish. You are going to do something you may prefer to do mindlessly and give it your full attention. After you become skillful at washing a dish mindfully you can try this exercise with any number of chores.

Choose a quiet moment to select a clean dish and place it in an empty sink. Just look at the dish for a moment and become aware of the color, shape and texture. You may become aware that other thoughts come into your mind while doing this exercise. This is inevitably going to happen because numerous thoughts come and go in our head all day, every day. Simply notice them, notice the tendency to fight them, and let them be. Gently bring yourself back to the task of focusing on the physical characteristics of the dish.

Now, pick up the dish and allow comfortably warm water to pass over it. Notice the sensations of the water, its temperature, and the feel of the dish as the water passes over it. Once again, you

are likely to notice a variety of thoughts that aren't related to this task. Simply notice them without judging them as good or bad, right or wrong, but simply an activity in your mind that comes and goes. The specific thoughts you are having do not matter, just your ability to notice and focus on the feelings and sensations that the water and the dish create.

Allow yourself to feel the sensations in more and more detail. In this way, you strengthen your concentration.

Now, wash the dish with soap and become aware of the additional sensation of smell and touch. As you continue to mindfully wash this dish, notice any sounds around you and any thoughts you are having as though they are simply words or pictures on a train going slowly by you and gently bring your attention back to the task of washing the dish. Remain in the moment with washing the dish and you will be able to increase your ability to control your focus.

Yoga For Self-Awareness

Mountain Pose. A mountain is steady, strong and still. The mountain can be a symbol of something to overcome or conquer—perhaps the climb towards a goal you want to achieve. The view from the top of a mountain can be exhilarating but you should enjoy the hike to the top as well.

Stand with your feet hip width apart. Press your feet firmly down into the earth. Your hands can be alongside the body or palms together at your heart. Lift your belly, head and heart. Your shoulders are back and down. Look straight ahead. Activate the muscles in your body. Hold for three to five breaths.

It can be difficult to stand in stillness and silence. However, it is important to give yourself this time to build your awareness of your mind and body.

As you hold this pose think about these questions:

1. What do I stand for?
2. What are my obstacles in life?
3. Am I centered in the present, too impatient, or holding back?

Cory Lund Photography

In-Between Chapters Mindfulness Exercises

1. Breathe Counting Exercise: Practice this daily.

2. Basic Centering Exercise: practice this every other day.

2. A Mindful Snack Exercise: practice this at least one time.

3. A Mindful Chore Exercise: practice this at least one time.

4. You can add any other mindfulness exercises you have learned: _____

You are starting to think about your thoughts and feelings
in a different way than you have before.

What I Have Learned About Myself And My Roller Derby Performance

In each chapter of this book, you are likely to learn a variety of new things about yourself and your derby performance. After you read each chapter, complete this form as soon as possible. The purpose of this is to ensure that you are learning and remembering the important concepts from each chapter.

1._____

_____

_____

2._____

_____

_____

3._____

_____

_____

4._____

_____

_____

5._____

_____

_____

5 VALUES

In this chapter we will explore the connection between values and value-driven actions. What are values? Values are what is truly important to us. Our roller derby values are the things that are important to us about this sport. When we let them, our roller derby values can guide our choices so that we are always on the right track and have a meaningful career. You began to explore your values when you answered the 'Why?' question in the goal setting chapter. Our values are why we want things. When we act according to these values, we not only do what we need to do to achieve our roller derby goals, we achieve our goals in a way that we can be proud of. These types of behaviors are called value-driven actions. Your roller derby values will be the foundation for the rest of this book.

> "Having fun is important because if you don't have fun you become this team that is really serious and focused way too much on the game. The whole entire point of roller derby is to have fun."
>
> —Vampire Bunny
>
> Age 11, Skating 4 years

My Roller Derby Story

Take some time to write down your roller derby story as if you are 20 years in the future and looking back. This activity will help you begin to identify your roller derby values.

My Roller Derby Story

Imagine your friends and family are sitting around the table and sharing stories about your roller derby career 20 years from now. How would you like your derby career and you as an athlete to be remembered? What kinds of things would you want to hear them say about you?

_____

_____

_____

_____

_____

_____

_____

_____

_____

_____

_____

_____

_____

_____

_____

Discover Your Roller Derby Values

Our roller derby values are at the very heart of why our goals in roller derby are important to us. We are reaching for our values in all that we do. Our values are at the heart of our intentions—they are why we want to achieve things. They are things that we really need and represent what is truly necessary to us. Our values can even provide direction and help us to make decisions when we need it.

So how do you figure out what your roller derby values are (we will simply refer to them as "values" from now on)? Think about the roller derby goal that you established in Chapter 2 and ask yourself, "Why is this important to me?" When you dig deeply enough you will arrive at your values. You might need to ask yourself the question more than once to get there. There are probably words you included in your Roller Derby Story that can give you clues as to what your values are. You may have already discovered your values during the goal setting exercise. Refer to the list of Values on the next page if you need ideas. An example of this process is below:

My Roller Derby Goal: *I want to improve my speed.*

Why is this important to me?

I like progressing in it. I don't want to feel that I'm at a standstill.

Why is this important to me? (Ask this question again to dig deeper)

It makes me feel like I'm accomplishing something. Like I'm successful.

My Value(s): *Accomplishment, Success*

My Roller Derby Values

My Roller Derby Goal:

Why is this important to me?

My Value(s):

Values

Belonging: Relationships are important to you. You want to feel loved and cared about.

Challenge: You enjoy taking on difficult tasks and problems.

Creativity: Having new ideas and able to adapt is important to you.

Contribution: Giving back and helping are important to you. You enjoy feeling like your part is needed.

Daring: Having the courage to take risks is important to you. You like to have an adventurous life with new and exciting experiences.

Determination: Putting a great deal of effort into everything you do is important to you. You stay committed and focused on what you set out to accomplish

Fun: Not taking things too seriously is important to you. You like laughing, playing and you value humor.

Gratitude: You are humble and appreciative of your gifts and opportunities.

Happiness: Feeling good is important to you. You treat your body and mind as best you can. You enjoy eating well, sleeping well, and being fit.

Honesty: Being truthful to yourself and others is important to you. Others can easily see what you want to represent.

Independence: Being able to make your own choices and not be controlled by others is important to you.

Justice: Being free of bias or injustice and treating ourselves and others equally is important to you.

Learning: You understand that we are always in a state of improvement. Making progress is important to you.

Loyalty: Supporting those you care about, committing yourselves to others and being faithful is important to you. You want the same in return.

Peace: Agreement rather than fighting is important to you

Responsibility: Taking care of things when it is in your power to do so is important to you.

Power: Having control over others is important to you.

Relaxation: Being comfortable, leisure time, and not working too hard is important to you.

Respect: Celebrating yourself and others is important to you. You honor individuality and differences.

Responsibility: You are accountable for the outcomes of your actions. You are dependable.

Safety: You don't want to be hurt (physically or emotionally). You are aware of physical and mental limitations. Security is important to you.

Simplicity: You often check to see if the simplest way works first. Not making things more difficult than they need to be is important to you. You have minimal needs.

Success: Being good at what you do is important to you. You like to accomplish what you set out to achieve.

Trust: You know this is an essential ingredient to successful relationships with teammates and coaches.

My Values Worksheet

After you come up with all of your roller derby values, use this worksheet to write down the things that could get in the way of being true to your value(s). Then write down what you need to add or change about your actions to be true to your value(s).

For Example:

My Goal: *I want to improve my speed.*

Why is this important to me?

I like progressing in it. I don't want to feel that I'm at a standstill.

Value(s) *Accomplishment, Success*

What could get in the way of being true to my value(s)? *Only focusing on the big things and not the little ways you're making progress like getting faster or jumping higher.*

What do I need to do more of or change to be true to my value(s)?

Everyday write down what I feel like I did good that day. Not give up. Have something to focus on at practice.

My Goal:

Why is this important to me?

Value(s):

What could get in the way of being true to my value(s)?

What do I need to do more of or change to be true to my value(s)?

Value-Driven VS. Emotion-Driven Actions

"When I'm jamming I feel like there is so much pressure on me. At practice I'll jam and I'll just laugh because I mess up. But in a game I feel like a weight is on me. Blocking I don't have as much pressure on me because there's three others out there."

—Tap Out

Age 13, Skating 3 ½ years

If we are not living a value-driven life, we are living an emotion-driven life. A value-driven life is when we make choices according to what really matters to us. When we act in ways that are in line with our values it's hard to go wrong. The alternative to acting in a value-driven way is to act in a way that is emotion-driven. To be emotion-driven means we make choices and decisions based on how we are feeling at any one time. The danger in this is the fleeting uncontrollable nature of emotions. They don't last and they come and go without our having to do anything. So if we respond according to how we are feeling at the time our actions are going to be inconsistent. Consistency is key to achieving your derby goals. Our values, on the other hand, typically don't change. So they are a much better basis for our actions. Acting in a value-driven way will increase the likelihood that your derby goals will be achieved.

When we are value-driven at practice and at games, and all the times in between, we are not only enhancing the possibility that we will enjoy the results of all of our hard work, but also the journey on the way to getting there. A good analogy for this is a road trip. Have you ever been on road trip where the only intention was to get to your destination as fast as possible? Was that trip enjoyable? Consider a different type of road trip where part of the goal was to pick out some interesting things to stop and do along the way. The second trip would be much more fun. That is what it means when people say to enjoy the journey, not just be focused on the destination. This is the secret to enjoying life and roller derby.

"I'm the cheerleader of the team because if we're having a tough bout I'm usually the one sitting because I'm not all the way there yet. So if they're frustrated I'm trying to cheer them up and make them laugh.

—Brozilla

Age 16, Skating 2 ½ years

In order to make sure we are making value-driven choices, we need to ask ourselves this question: "Would I be acting like this if I was in a different mood?"

Emotions serve the purpose of allowing us to fully experience all that life has to offer. Emotions can be difficult to endure (fear, worry, anger, frustration, anxiety) or wonderful (joy, pride, happiness, excitement). Some of the emotions we consider to be negative may make us feel uncomfortable or even terrible. Most people try to feel less of the negative feelings and more of the positive ones. We should not try to avoid or control even the most upsetting emotions because they contribute to our overall life experience.

Some emotions become barriers to achieving our goals. Can you think of which emotions get in the way of your success? In which situations do you feel these emotions? What actions typically follow these emotions? It is important to realize that it is not the emotions that are the problem, it is the way we respond to them.

My goals are what I want
to achieve in this sport.
My values tell me why
my goals are important to me.
My value-driven actions are how
I am going to stay true to
my values while I achieve my goals.

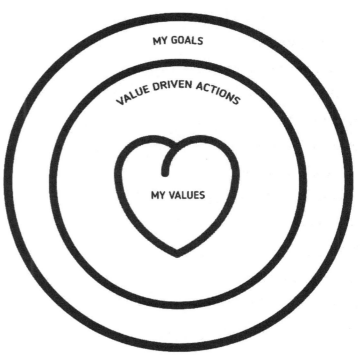

Direct vs. Indirect Emotions

Another important thing to learn about emotions is the concept of direct and indirect emotions. A direct emotion is one that is appropriately related to a situation. An example of this is a skater may feel sad that she wasn't selected for the travel team. The sadness is an appropriate feeling to have in response to the situation. She worked hard for something and wanted it really badly and it is disappointing when it doesn't happen.

An indirect emotion comes in response to the thoughts in our minds, not anything in reality. To go back to the skater in our travel team example—she initially felt sad that she wasn't selected but then became angry. The anger came in response to the thoughts in her mind, not anything in reality. The sadness triggered beliefs she had about herself and life such as, *Nothing ever goes my way* or *I wasn't treated fairly.* These thoughts brought on feelings of anger. Anger was an indirect emotion and sadness was a direct emotion. Sadness was related to the situation and anger was related indirectly to the situation. Does it seem silly to let an emotion that is not even directly related to the situation get in the way of our being our best?

Sometimes the indirect, or secondary, emotions serve the purpose of helping us to avoid feeling bad. Emotions such as sadness, doubt, and fear can be experienced as a weak or vulnerable feeling. On the other hand, emotions such as anger can be experienced as a strong or powerful feeling which can be easier to deal with. Sometimes we develop responses to avoid feeling uncomfortable emotions and these become automatic patterns that we are not even aware of. Then when we feel negative emotions our automatic responses are triggered or set into motion.

"I got scared and avoided trying new things. I've avoided going the extra mile. Sometimes I'm too empowered and I get cocky."

Ginger Slap

Age 15, Skating 4 years

Positive and Negative Emotions

Make a list of the positive and negative emotions you experience as a result of your involvement in roller derby. Circle the emotions that are barriers to your performance.

Positive Emotions	Negative Emotions

What I Have Given Up For Emotions Form

The purpose of this form is to help you become more aware of what you have given up to control, change or avoid your emotions. How is this affecting your ability to be a great performer and/or enjoy roller derby?

In the first column, list a situation related to practice or competition that triggered a strong emotion. In the second column, write down the specific emotion and thought you experienced. In the third column, record what you did to control, change or avoid your emotion. In the fourth column, write down what effect your efforts to control, change or avoid your emotion had on you. In the last column, write down the long-term consequences of your efforts to rid yourself of these emotions (what you gave up to reduce or satisfy your emotion).

Complete form beneath example provided below:

Situation or event	Emotion and Thought	What you did to control emotion	Short-term effect	Long-term consequence
Criticized by coach	Angry and thought over and over about him being a jerk	Stayed quiet and took an "I don't care" attitude. Thought about friends.	Felt less angry, but uninvolved the next day	Looked even worse in coach's eyes, didn't practice well, looked like I was pouting, didn't further my goals

Painting With The Breath Mindfulness Exercise

This exercise will help you expand your mindfulness skills and allow you to work on self-awareness and attention.

Find a comfortable sitting position. Notice the position of your body, particularly your legs, hands, and feet. Allow your eyes to close gently.

Take several deep breaths and notice the air going in and out of your body. Notice the sound and feel of your own breathing as you breathe in and out. Allow your focus of attention to be on your belly rising and falling with each breath.

As you continue to breathe in and out, imagine that there is a paintbrush in your hand and that you are painting a stroke upward with each inhale and then a stroke downward with each exhale. Imagine the picture that these strokes would create.

> "I probably could have jammed during a crucial moment in my roller derby career but I gave up. I felt like I couldn't in my mind. Looking back, I think I probably could have. Even trying would have been better than giving up. It was horrible. I stopped and started crying. I had never had to try that hard. I told myself that "I lost." I was thinking about how tired I was and how I couldn't understand why I couldn't do what I wanted to do. If only I would have gotten up, stopped crying and kept jamming."
>
> —Slim Reaper
>
> Age 16, Skating 7 years

As you slowly continue to breathe in and out, notice that you may become aware of a variety of thoughts and emotions that enter and leave your mind. Simply notice them as though they are waves slowly hitting a shore, gently allow them to flow in and back out, and once again focus on your breathing and all the sensations that come. Having a variety of thoughts and emotions is not incorrect or in any way a problem, but simply reflects the reality of the human mind. There is no need to change, fix or attempt to control these experiences. Simply note the passing thoughts in your mind and refocus on your breathing.

Allow yourself to continue to breathe gently in and out, focusing your thoughts on the physical sensations of each breath that your take. Whenever you are ready, slowly open your eyes and become fully aware of your surroundings.

Simple Roller Derby-Related Mindfulness Activity

Now you are going to plan to do your first roller derby-related mindfulness activity. Think of a simple activity that you can easily do without paying much attention. Warm-up laps, pre-practice stretching, or gearing up are all good ideas. In being mindful, you will focus your attention completely on the task instead of doing it mindlessly. Being mindful means your body and mind are in the same place.

"Frightened and scared are mostly in my head. I always think that I can't do it even though I probably can. And I think it will hurt even though it won't. I will do it and I kind of stop or I will do it half-heartedly."

—Lucky Harms

Age 13, Skating 4 years

Your goals in completing this activity are to be able to:

- Observe and describe your thoughts, feelings and actions.

- Observe and describe what is going on in your surroundings.

- Be in the moment.

- Be nonjudgmental (don't think of anything occurring internally or externally as being good or bad).

- Notice if your mind drifts away from the task and gently bring it back.

Yoga For Growth

Tree Pose. Trees provide us with fruit to eat, shade to rest in, paper to write on, branches to climb and wood for our homes. Trees are homes to many creatures great and small. The longer a tree lives, the more layers it puts on. Trees are connected to the earth and reach for the sky. If their roots aren't deep enough they will tumble over.

The tree pose energizes, focuses attention and is good for posture. Stand with your feet together. Shift your weight onto your left foot. Slowly bend your right knee and draw your right foot up, placing the sole as high as possible on the inner leg without strain (ankle, shin or thigh). Activate your body and press standing leg down, rooting yourself like a tree to the earth. Press palms together at your heart center. Then breathe in and stretch arms and head up like branches towards the sky. Finding something outside yourself to focus on will help you to stay balanced. Hold for three to five breaths. Repeat on other leg.

While you are in tree pose consider the following:

1. When am I solid like an oak and when do I waver like a willow?

2. How am I branching out?

3. In which areas do I need to grow?

Eric Lyons Photography

In-Between Chapters Mindfulness Exercises:

1. Breathe Counting Exercise: Practice this daily.

2. Painting With The Breath Exercise: Practice this every other day.

3. You can add any other mindfulness exercises you have learned: _____

_____

4. Simple Roller Derby-Related Mindfulness Activity: _____

_____

Now that you understand what is truly important to you,
you can begin to get all of your actions to be in line with your values.

What I Have Learned About Myself And My Roller Derby Performance

In each chapter of this book, you are likely to learn a variety of new things about yourself and your derby performance. After you read each chapter, complete this form as soon as possible. The purpose of this is to ensure that you are learning and remembering the important concepts from each chapter.

1._____

_____

_____

2._____

_____

_____

3._____

_____

_____

4._____

_____

_____

5._____

_____

_____

6 ACCEPTANCE

This chapter will expand on the concept of poise which was introduced in Chapter 3. You will also learn more about how trying to avoid feeling negative emotions or thinking negative thoughts can actually hurt your game, rather than help it. Accepting that sometimes you are going to think and feel badly is an important step on the way to learning to focus on the task at hand rather than on what's going on in your head.

3-2-1 Centering Exercise

"You feel happy being out there with everyone but sometimes you feel a little angry at everyone."

—Vampire Bunny

Age 11, Skating 4 years

To be centered, or grounded, means to be fully in the present moment. This centering exercise is a quick and easy way to get out of your head. It can be used when you notice you are thinking about unhelpful or negative things. To try this out, think about something upsetting that happened to you at a game or practice recently. Once you have it in your head, follow the instructions on the next page. When you are done you will feel grounded and focused on your immediate surroundings rather than stuck on your thoughts.

1. What are three things that you can see?

What are three things that you can touch?

What are three things that you can hear?

2. What are two things that you can see

(they can be the same things as in step 1)?

What are two things that you can touch?

What are two things that you can hear?

3. What is one thing that you can see?

What is one thing that you can touch?

What is one thing that you can hear?

Cory Lund Photography

One Minute Hearing Exercise

Close your eyes and take one minute to hear, without judging, all of the sounds that may be happening around you. Simply, notice the sounds and notice any thoughts that these sounds trigger. If you notice your mind is no longer paying attention to the sounds around you, gently refocus.

Connecting Mindfulness and Acceptance

By now you have been practicing mindfulness for about three weeks. Can you now notice when you are doing something without being mindful? Most find mindfulness to be a useful skill to apply to many parts of life, not just roller derby. Mindfulness can help us pay attention in class, be mentally present in conversations with others, be more aware and appreciative of our surroundings—lots of things! When we approach anything in a mindful way we can experience it more fully and enjoy it more.

"Before a game some of the other team were talking crap about us and said 'we can beat you' and I just smiled and walked away."

-Irene Yonek

Age 14, Skating 5 years

Practicing mindfulness will allow you to be able to observe your thoughts and feelings without judging them. You will be able to step back a bit from the things in your mind and just notice them without needing to immediately react. When our thoughts and feelings aren't influencing us it makes it much easier to accept any type of thought or feeling—even ones that we consider bad or uncomfortable.

"If there are big girls out there who are hitting big hits I will purposefully sit at the end of the bench so I won't have to go out there and jam."

—Tap Out

Age 13, Skating 3 ½ years

Often we blame our actions on our how we are feeling at any given time. For example, we may say things like:

"*I yelled at her because I was angry.*"
"*I didn't try that jump because I was scared.*"
"*I treated my coach disrespectfully because I was irritated.*"

When we say things like that we are acknowledging that our emotions have power over us. We are letting them drive us. This process can get in the way of staying true to your values and reaching your roller derby goals. Using the examples above we can look at how living an emotion-driven life can get in the way of how we truly want to be:

<table>
<tr><td>If we value being a good sport, we want to treat opposing team members well. If we want to further our skating skills, we need to take calculated risks. If we value being a member of a team, we need to listen to our coaches, respect them and trust them.</td><td>"I feel excited and happy when we win or after somebody compliments me when I do something on the track. After I do a 30-point jam."

—The Crusher

Age 16, Skating 6 years</td></tr>
</table>

Emotions aren't what's getting in the way of you being the best skater you can be. Reacting to emotions in ways that take you away from your values and goals is the problem. Emotions are not the problem. Emotions, good or bad, are a part of this crazy, roller derby experience and are what makes it so amazing. Accept that sometimes you will feel bad along your journey. Disappointment, regret, jealousy, anger, fear, sadness, frustration, doubt…these are all a part of the ride. Don't try to avoid, control or eliminate negative thoughts and feelings. Thoughts and emotions come and go if we let them. Accepting that all kinds of thoughts and feelings will be a part of your roller derby experience—from ultimate joy to crushing defeat—will help you to act in ways that are true to your values, rather than driven by your emotions.

Choose to live in the great moments for as long as you can.

An emotion-driven life means always trying to feel good and avoid feeling bad. When we run away from situations where we might end up feeling bad it can get in the way of advancing in roller derby. You may do things like:

- Choose to practice something you are already good at rather than a more challenging activity so you feel accomplished.

- Skip practice after a fight with a teammate because you don't want to feel mad again.

- Only volunteer to jam when you see that the opposing team's blockers are at a lower skill level than you so you don't have to risk feeling embarrassed.

Doing all of these types of things keeps you from being the best skater you can be. We need to challenge ourselves, attend practice, face fears and risk feeling badly in order to advance our skills. Can you think of some situations where trying to feel good or avoid feeling bad caused you to do things that hurt your roller derby career instead of helping it?

Living an emotion-driven life can also get in the way of being true to our values. When we act only in response to how we are feeling emotionally our behaviors are not always going to align with what is really important to us. We may end up acting in ways that are unpredictable or in ways that we regret. We may respond in ways that are way over the top at times or not even care other times. You may do things like:

- Be unsupportive of a teammate's success because you feel jealous.

- Be friendly to fresh meat only on days when you are in a good mood.

- Say 'thank you' to compliments only when you feel good about your performance and deny them otherwise.

"One time I was given the jam pantie and someone flat out said I wasn't going to be able to do it so that pissed me off. But I pushed myself to do it and gave it 100% and was able to get through and I was like 'yay!'"

—Brozilla

Age 16, Skating 2 ½ years

Poise

If you are always acting in response to how you are feeling or thinking at any given time your efforts towards success are going to be inconsistent. You will only do the things necessary for success when you *feel* like doing them, rather than doing what it takes no matter how you are feeling or thinking.

To put a consistent effort into your skating all the time you will need to transform the belief, "I want to skate well *but* I am angry, frustrated, or sad" to "I want to skate well *and* I am angry, frustrated, or sad." The first statement shows emotion-driven actions and the second shows value-driven actions.

> "I get caught up in not being good enough sometimes because I'm the oldest and some of the younger people are better than me."
>
> —Ally Oops
>
> Age 17, Skating 4 years

Poise means being balanced and in-control in the face of the difficult emotions that are a part of the intense sport of roller derby. If you use your values as your guide when choosing your actions and making your decisions, it will help you stay on the right track. Accepting all thoughts and feelings, even the ones you consider to be bad, painful or wrong will help you to act in a values-directed way.

Often we choose feeling better in the moment over what is the best choice for the long run. Picture a tall mountain. Imagine your values are at the top this mountain. During your climb to the top of the mountain, you may experience all kinds of negative thoughts and emotions. You may doubt you can do it, you may put yourself down, you may compare yourself to others who are climbing faster than you, you may question whether or not you should even be climbing this mountain. You may feel fear, worry, frustration, sadness, or anger. If you listen to the things your mind is telling you as if they are the truth you would quit climbing. If you acted as if your emotions were your guide you would turn back. Quitting your climb or turning back would help you to feel better in the moment, but you would be no closer to your goals or living up to your values. If you kept focusing on what you needed to do to get to the top, you would make progress upward. This is poise in action.

Distress Tolerance

Think of a stressful or difficult roller derby situation. Notice the effect that thinking about this event has on your body. These sensations don't need to be controlled or lessened. Simply notice these feelings and allow them to co-exist with the moment. This is what the skill of distress tolerance is all about. Being able to tolerate the negative thoughts, emotions and bodily sensations that go along with being involved in roller derby is part of being poised. You need to be able to do what you need to do no matter how you are thinking or feeling—no matter what is going on in your head. This is the ultimate definition of mental toughness.

"I got expelled from the whole building. When I was going to the box people on their bench were yelling at me and I just turned around and started flipping people off. I was only thinking of anger and not about what could happen afterwards. I could have lost my whole season and if I would have hit someone I could have gotten in trouble."

—Kick N Ash

Age 15, Skating 6 years

Practice distress tolerance by imagining that you have just experienced the following scenarios. First read each scenario. Next, put yourself into the situation by really thinking and feeling in a way that you would typically. After that, sit with the emotions without trying to change them, make them go away or control them in any way. Finally, gently shift your focus to something outside yourself in order to reset and get centered in the present moment. You can use the 3-2-1 Centering Exercise you learned earlier in the book if needed.

Scenario 1:

Your teammate just announced that she made it onto an elite competitive team that you had also tried out for but didn't make.

What would you be thinking and feeling?

Scenario 2:

You've been close to beating 33 laps in 5 minutes but just skated only 29.

What would you be thinking and feeling?

Scenario 3:

It's the last jam of the game and you get called out on a penalty you don't think you committed.

What are you thinking and feeling?

There are two connected foundations of elite performance in sports:

1. Being fully in the moment

2. Poise

Being able to fully pay attention to the moment will ensure that your focus is 100% where it needs to be. Our minds can only completely focus on one thing at a time and you can learn how to determine where your focus needs to be in order to do the best job possible. You can also learn to shift your focus as needed for each changing roller derby situation. This book is helping you to build your foundation for elite performance through the practice of **mindfulness**, **acceptance** of the negative thoughts and feelings that are inherent in this sport and a **commitment** to taking the actions necessary to stay true to your values.

You need to be able to do what you need to do no matter how you are thinking or feeling. This is the ultimate definition of mental toughness.

Cory Lund Photography

Emotion And Performance Interference Form

Write down performance situations that happened recently, the emotions you experienced, the intensity of the emotions, the degree to which the emotions interfered with your roller derby performance, and how the emotion interfered with your roller derby performance.

Complete the form beneath the example provided below:

Situation	Emotion (Rate intensity 1 to 10)	Performance Interference (Rate intensity 1 to 10)	How did the emotion interfere with your performance?
Coach said I wasn't working as hard as another skater.	*Sad, frustrated* 7	9	*Thought about quitting sport, felt like coach didn't appreciate my hard work.*

Conflicting Feelings Activity

This activity can help you accept and honor conflicting feelings. This is an activity you can do on your own, however it is more effective to do with your teammates.

Imagine that it is the last jam of the game and your team is behind by one point. Your coach has just asked you to jam. You have two conflicting feelings that are speaking very loudly to you inside your body. What are they?

If you are doing this activity on your own write down each of the feelings on a piece of paper and put them side by side. Think of what each of the feelings are saying to you. Try to come up with at least five responses for each feeling and write them down. For example:

Excitement

"Yay! It's going to be so great to help your team win!"

Fear

"Don't do it, you're going to mess up!"

Which voice should you obey? What action would that choice lead to? Now come up with ways you can listen to both feelings. Write the solutions down.

If you are doing this activity with your team, have the group come up with the list of responses each feeling is saying. Then ask a volunteer to be the skater with the dilemma. This person will stand up. Ask two more skaters to play the parts of each feeling. Have them stand on either side of the first skater and say out loud what their feeling is saying to him or her. Then ask the rest of the group to help come up with solutions that honor both feelings.

This activity helps teach you that feelings are not bad—they are just warning systems from the body. What would life be like if we only listened to fear or only listened to joy or any other single feeling?

Try this activity several times with other situations you and/or your teammates can think of!

> "One time someone had pantie passed me and I went to the box. The jam right after that I was extremely pissed beyond control. We just got in a huddle and we said "yeah we're 60 points behind" and we played the hardest we ever had. I had to calm down and focus not just on myself."
>
> —Ginger Slap
>
> Age 15, Skating 4 years

Yoga For Tolerance

Yoga can teach us many things that we can apply to roller derby and life. One of the things it can teach us is to be able to recognize the difference between discomfort and pain. Pain is a red, sharp feeling that can lead to injury. Discomfort is brown and dull. Our breath is the tie that helps us connect feeling to thinking and mind to body, so we can develop the ability to make accurate choices about what we are experiencing.

Yoga can also teach us to be able to tolerate the discomfort that is a part of learning and growing and living. If you want to stretch a tight muscle, you should go directly into a pose that stretches and opens that muscle and breath into it, not around it. Breathe into the discomfort. Coexist with it rather than avoid it. If you want to stretch out of your comfort zone in roller derby you need to approach it in the same way. This is the way you will become stronger and more flexible in body, mind and action.

Let's practice this process with a simple yoga pose, the Seated Forward Bend.

Seated Forward Bend. Sit on the floor with your legs straight in front of you. Inhale, raising your arms up and then exhale, leaning forward from the hip, not the waist. Keep the back long, reaching forward rather than rounding the back. Reach your hands forward just until you feel the stretch but not beyond. Your hands may end up as far as your shins, touching your feet, or further, depending on your flexibility. Hold the pose for a little while, breathing into any place where you feel discomfort.

"I always feel really nervous before games even though I know we're going to win. I always feel butterflies but that always makes me try harder. That makes them go away. The harder I push it just goes up then it all goes away."

—Lucky Harms

Age 13, Skating 4 years

When you are ready to stretch further, don't forcefully pull or push your body into the forward bend. Instead, lengthen your upper body into the pose, keeping your head raised. With an inhale, lift and lengthen, with each exhale, move a little more fully into the forward bend. In this way you are moving and stretching further and further, almost unnoticeably, along with each breath.

While in this pose, think about the following questions:

1. Who do I need to be more tolerant of?

2. Can I accept my imperfections?

3. What is holding me back?

Just Breathe.

Extension Of The Roller Derby-Related Mindfulness Activity

Now you are going to plan to extend your roller derby-related mindfulness activity to something a little bit more complicated than the last one. Think of an activity that takes some paying attention to be able to be successful but something you are pretty confident in. Some ideas are jumps, transitions, falls, stops and skating backwards. You will focus your attention completely on the task, being mindful, with your head and body in the same place. Your goals in completing this activity will be the same as with the simple roller derby-related mindfulness activity—to be able to:

- Determine what you should be focusing on in order to be successful at this task.

- Notice if your mind drifts away from the task and gently bring it back.

- Be in the moment.

- Be nonjudgmental (don't think of anything going on in your head or around you as being good or bad).

In-Between Chapters Mindfulness Exercises:

1. Breath Counting Exercise: Practice this daily.

2. Painting The Breath Exercise: Practice this at least one time.

2. 3-2-1 Centering Exercise: Practice this at least two times.

3. You can add any other mindfulness exercises you have learned: _____

    _____

4. Extension of the Roller Derby-Related Mindfulness Activity: _____

    _____

You accept that negative, as well as positive experiences,

are a part of the roller derby journey.

What I Have Learned About Myself And My Roller Derby Performance

In each chapter of this book, you are likely to learn a variety of new things about yourself and your derby performance. After you read each chapter, complete this form as soon as possible. The purpose of this is to ensure that you are learning and remembering the important concepts from each chapter.

1._____

_____

_____

2._____

_____

_____

3._____

_____

_____

4._____

_____

_____

5._____

_____

_____

7 COMMITMENT

In this chapter you will continue to work on understanding the difference between goals and values. Goals are the destination you want to get to. Values are how you want to get there. We are also going to continue to look at which thoughts and emotions have been barriers to consistently taking the actions necessary to achieve your goals.

As you learned from completing the Emotions and Performance Interference Form, emotion-driven choices, rather than value-driven choices are the real reasons for having difficulties reaching your roller derby goals, not the emotions themselves. When we experience negative thoughts and emotions, we sometimes react to those experiences in ways that take us away from our goals. The core skills of mindfulness and acceptance can help you to take actions that are true to your values, rather than being led by your emotions. The goal is to eventually be able to disconnect your actions and choices from your emotions. Living in a way that is true to your values takes you towards your roller derby goals.

Emotion-driven choices will change
depending on our mood.
Value-driven choices are more consistent.

> "I don't want to quit. Because derby is kind of my safety net meaning it's something I can do to take my mind off things like it's a stress reliever."
>
> -Irene Yonek
>
> Age 14, Skating 5 years

One-Minute Seeing Exercise

Pick one object around you to focus on. It could be anything that isn't moving like a book, a vase or a pen. Take one minute to stay focused on it for as long as you can. Silently observe as many details about the object as you can. Take note of its color, size, texture, etc. If you realize that you are thinking of something else other than the object, gently shift your attention back. Try to hold your attention to the object for as long as possible. When the minute is over, think about whether it was difficult to hold your attention on one thing for that long.

This was an exercise in task-focused attention. That means being able to sustain or hold your focus or attention to one thing for a long period of time. You will become more skilled at this with practice.

Connecting Values, Goals And Actions

There is a subtle but clear difference between motivation and commitment. While motivation means simply wanting something, commitment means consistently doing the things that are going to get you there.

Cory Lund Photography

The mountain symbol mentioned earlier is great for illustrating the connection between our values, goals and actions. Our values are high up on this mountain. They are what is important to us about this sport and what we want to honor by our actions. These are the things we are really reaching for. The path that leads up the mountain is made from our value-driven actions. By staying true to your values, you will also increase the chance that you will achieve your goals and have a meaningful career in this sport. Emotion-driven actions will not take us up the mountain and may even take us away from achieving our goals. Our roller derby goals are "how" we are going to measure our success in this sport and "what" we are going to accomplish, but our values are "why" it matters to us.

> "Show up to practice, be respectful to everyone on my team. Show that I want a place on this team. Don't argue with girls over stupid stuff that doesn't even matter."
>
> —The Crusher
>
> Age 16, Skating 6 years

As an example, if your value is success, then your value-driven actions need to reflect that. Some actions you will need to take to be successful in roller derby are attend practice regularly, try your best and listen to your coach. If your roller derby goal is to be a harder hitter, then committing to your value-driven actions will ultimately help you to achieve this. Below is another example:

> "That I gave it my all."
>
> —Blackheart Blockher
>
> Age 14, Skating 4 years

Roller derby goal: *To be a starting lineup skater for my team.*

Why is this important to me?

I want to be so good I'm competitive at every aspect. I want people to see all the hard work I put in is showing.

Related value: *Notoriety*

What could get in the way of this happening (emotion-driven action)?

Embarrassment, worries about not doing well. Turning down opportunities to skate with other teams.

What do you need to do more of or change to make this happen (value-driven action)?

Take advantage of opportunities to skate as much as possible.

Safety   Challenge   Trust   Independance   Creativity

Health   Responsibility   Fun   Bravery

Fairness   Love

Respect   Belonging   Success

Security   Loyalty   Risk

Being Real

Values Mountain

Path= Value-Driven Actions, Trees= Goals

(Adapted from Casey Jackson's Focus Mountain)

Committing To Values

Are you ready to commit to your values? This means accepting whatever negative thoughts or feelings you may experience along the way. Recall that the whole range of emotions, from sorrow to joy, are a part of being human. A variety of emotions allow us to experience life. Committing to your values also means

"Always talk to your teammates and don't be a loner in the corner."

—Vampire Bunny

Age 11, Skating 4 years

you may have to face your fears or take other actions that seem like the opposite of what your automatic urge is. For example, if your value is Friendship then you may have to be kind to someone who irritates you when your automatic urge is to ignore them or be rude to them.

A funny way to think about this phenomenon is to make a comparison to a cat stuck in a tree. The cat wants to get out of the tree (her goal) because she values Safety but she doesn't take the steps needed to get her where she wants to go. She gets caught up in her emotion (fear) and thoughts (*Everyone needs to stay away from me!*) and does not see the bigger picture. The cat may even do the opposite of what is going to take her towards her goal, such as scratch someone trying to help her or climb even higher. If she took value-driven actions she would do what she needed to do in order to get out of the tree, even if that meant feeling fear or accepting help.

> "I've gotten frustrated and I've pushed harder and I've gotten through."
>
> —Ally Oops
>
> Age 17, Skating 4 years

Instead of **FEAR**:

Fusion with your thoughts. Don't treat your thoughts and feelings as if they are absolute truths.

Evaluation of experience. Don't judge certain thoughts and feelings as negative or bad.

Avoidance of experience. Don't try to control, avoid or react to "bad" feelings such as fear, sadness and frustration.

Reason-giving for your behavior. Don't say things like, "I did it because I was angry."

ACT instead:

Accept your emotions. Accept that both good and bad feelings are part of the richness of life.

Choose a valued direction. Choose to stay focused on what is important to you about roller derby.

Take action. Make a commitment to take the actions that show this.

Approach, rather than avoid

Committing To Values Exercise

Roller Derby Goal:

Value(s):

Actions Needed To Be True To Your Value(s) (These are your value-driven actions):

1.

2.

3.

Are you willing to **commit** to taking the actions necessary to stay true to your values and achieve your goals? This means **accepting** whatever discomfort your mind and body may experience along the way.

Building Confidence

"Less of using words. I used to have a potty mouth and be really mean. If somebody would say something to me I would just lose it. Focusing more on what I need to do and not what other people want me to do."

—Kick N Ash

Age 15, Skating 6 years

Let's take a moment to check in on where you're at regarding your confidence that you will achieve your roller derby goals.

Rate the following questions on a scale from 1 to 10 with 10 being the highest:

As of right now, how important is it for you to achieve your roller derby goals?

    1   2   3   4   5   6   7   8   9   10

As of right now, how confident are you that you will achieve your roller derby goals?

    1   2   3   4   5   6   7   8   9   10

As of right now, where are you in terms of commitment and taking real, actual steps towards achieving your roller derby goals?

    1   2   3   4   5   6   7   8   9   10

If you rated yourself low on importance or commitment, then it is likely you did not select a roller derby goal that is in line with your values (what is most important to you). For example, if your goal is to make travel team but your value is Fun or Belonging, then the social aspects of being involved in derby may be more important to you than your other values—Accomplishment or Competition. That is going to make it tough for you to really put in the hard work necessary to

> "I value skills. Strength. I value my team and my friends even if they're forced to be with me."
>
> —Slim Reaper
>
> Age 16, Skating 7 years

make a select team. Sometimes one of our values is more important to us than another and will take priority in certain decisions we make about our lives. Through the process of self-awareness, we can learn to sort all of this out and set goals and take actions that are best for us.

If your importance and commitment are high but your confidence is low, complete the following items:

This is why I want to achieve my roller derby goal (If you don't have many good reasons you may need to rethink your goal):

1.

2.

3.

These are my strengths that will help me to achieve my roller derby goal:

1.

2.

3.

These are my skills and abilities that will help me to achieve my roller derby goal:

1.

2.

3.

These are my past successes related to my roller derby goal:

1.

2.

3.

Think of three things that will increase your confidence and write them below:

1.

2.

3.

Now rate your confidence again:

As of right now, how confident are you that you will achieve your roller derby goals?

| 1 | 2 | 3 | 4 | 5 | 6 | 7 | 8 | 9 | 10 |

Your confidence rating should have increased. Now you have a roller derby goal that is important to you, more confidence that you can achieve it and are committed to doing what it takes to get there! You will learn more about building confidence in chapter 10.

"I like control. I don't have a lot of control over myself. I'm a teenager and I don't have that much control over my life. In roller derby I can be as loud as possible and still work really well with everyone else. I like having that control."
—Ginger Slap

Age 15, Skating 4 years

DARN CAT

You must have a **D**esire to achieve your goal, an **A**bility to achieve your goal, a **R**eason to achieve your goal, and a **N**eed to achieve your goal in order to **C**ommit to **A**ction and **T**ake the steps to get there!

Photo by Daisy Norris

Roller-Derby Related Mindfulness Activity

Next you will plan to apply mindfulness to a different roller derby-related task. Think of another thing that you need to pay attention to in order to be successful but something you are pretty confident in. Some ideas are side surfing, grapevines and toe stop running. You will focus your attention completely on the task, being mindful, with your head and body in the same place. Your goals in completing this activity will be to be able to:

- Determine what you should be focusing on in order to be successful at this task
- Notice if your mind drifts away from the task and gently bring it back
- Be in the moment
- Be nonjudgmental (don't think of anything going on in your head or around you as being good or bad)

Yoga For Promise

Bow Pose. Wisdom says that hitting the bullseye is the result of flying one hundred arrows. The bow and arrow has been used for warfare and is also used to hunt—providing food that sustains life. When cupid hits your heart with an arrow, will you fall in love? A bow that is admired with wonder is the rainbow. A rainbow can be seen after a rain, when the sun re-emerges.

Lie on your belly. Bend your knees, reach back and grab your ankles. Pull your knees toward each other so they are hip width apart. Inhale, press feet back, lift chest and head up. As your legs, chest and head lift up, the movement looks like a bow, bent and aimed at the target. Keep breathing!

When working with this pose, consider the following:

1. How can I keep my aim straight?

2. How far should I bend?

3. Is there something I need to let go of?

In-Between Chapters Mindfulness Exercises:

Continue to practice mindfulness on a regular basis. Mindfulness helps you to focus your attention, be in the present moment, have awareness of your thoughts, feelings and actions and create distance between yourself and your thoughts and feelings. These are all elements needed to skate your best.

1. Breathe Counting Exercise: Practice this daily.

2. You can add any other mindfulness exercises you have learned. Which are your favorites?

_____

_____

2. Roller Derby-Related Mindfulness Activity: _____

_____

You are committed to actions that are aligned with your values.

What I Have Learned About Myself And My Roller Derby Performance

In each chapter of this book, you are likely to learn a variety of new things about yourself and your derby performance. After you read each chapter, complete this form as soon as possible. The purpose of this is to ensure that you are learning and remembering the important concepts from each chapter.

1._____

_____

_____

2._____

_____

_____

3._____

_____

_____

4._____

_____

_____

5._____

_____

_____

8 POISE

In this chapter you will be able to start being more flexible in how you respond to certain situations. This will allow you to react in helpful ways that will take you towards your goals instead of being stuck repeating the unhelpful things that you may have done in the past. Recall, poise is the ability to do what is in the best interest of your values and goals regardless of your thoughts and emotions. To be poised is to be in control of your actions, no matter what.

Yoga For Focus

Yoga can help us to train our focus because many of the poses require our full attention in order to be able to do them well. It is a great way to be able to experience the benefits of having your mind and body in the same place.

Here is a yoga pose that will help you to improve your ability to focus:

Eagle Pose. Eagles are a symbol of pride, power and victory. They are birds of prey that are known for their excellent sight—they can spot a snake or a mouse from high above. Eagles are often thought of as the king of the birds.

From standing, bend your knees slightly. Lift your left leg off the floor and cross your left knee tightly over your right knee. Hug your foot into your shin or hook the toes of your left foot behind your right calf. Spread your arms like wings and take them overhead. Bend your elbows and hook your left elbow

under your right elbow in front of your heart. Point your thumbs toward your nose and grab your right palm with your left hand. Your palms will be facing each other. Lift your elbows up and stretch your fingers towards the sky. Find a focal point to help you balance. Hold for three to five breaths. Repeat on the other side.

"That I was really nice and I was very good. I got through. I got the job done."

—Lucky Harms

Age 13, Skating 4 years

Getting into this position can be tough. You may feel awkward, unsteady and wrapped like a pretzel. Yet, when this pose is achieved, it is possible to concentrate with the single-pointedness of an eagle's vision.

While holding the eagle pose, think about the following:

1. What are some words that come to my mind when I think about an eagle?

2. What would it feel like to fly?

3. What am I proud of?

Danny Ngan Photography

Focus Training Exercise I

This exercise in task-focused attention (the ability to focus your attention on one thing for a long period of time) will help you develop the capacity to redirect attention away from the self (internal experiences such as thoughts like "*How am I doing?*" and feelings such as anxiety) and onto the relevant task at hand during difficult situations. Focus training can enhance mindfulness practice by helping us to keep our attention where we want it to be for longer and longer periods of time. This is an exercise you will need to do with a partner.

1. Sit with your back to your partner, so that no eye contact can occur. Your partner will then tell you a short story. The story can be about whatever the teller wants. If the story teller needs some ideas, there are a few short stories in the Appendix in the back of the book. Your job is just to listen and concentrate on the story. When the story is complete, you will have to retell story in as much detail as possible.

2. Next face the story teller and listen to another story while maintaining eye contact. Again, when the story is over you will retell the story, remembering as much detail as possible.

3. Then *you* are going to tell a story about a recent stressful, derby performance-related event. Include lots of thoughts, feelings and details. Tell a story that made you feel so upset at the time that you will easily be able to re-experience the same emotions. When you are done, your partner will immediately tell a new story and you will have to recall the details.

The goal of this exercise is to:

1. Help you gently move your attention from thoughts, feelings and bodily sensations to focus outside of yourself. You are moving your focus to what is necessary to being able to successfully complete the task at hand (in this case retelling a story).

2. Allow you to see that even with anxiety, frustration or other negative emotion you can focus attention as needed for the task at hand.

You can create your own roller derby-related focus training exercises such as these:

- See how long you can hold your attention on what the coach is saying to you.

- Watch another skater on your team that you admire. Focus fully on his or her movements.

- Set your skate in front of you and silently describe what you are seeing.

Opposite-Actions!

Developing or increasing poise requires you to confront difficult emotionally-charged situations and act in a way that is often the complete opposite of how you want to respond. You have to move towards what may cause you to experience negative emotions rather than to avoid them. You may discover that the actions that help you to act in the service of your values are often the opposite of what you automatically have the urge to do when you are acting to avoid experiencing certain emotions. These "approach" actions will align with your values instead of giving you short-term relief from stress.

In the chart below are some examples of emotions, the emotion's action urge and the helpful (value-driven) opposite action.

Letting go.

Opposite Action Chart		
Emotion	**Emotion's Action Urge**	**Opposite Action**
Sad	Be alone, be quiet, not participate	Join in with others, get active
Angry	Yell, be hurtful, attack	Be extra kind, no judgments, gently avoid
Frustrated	Give up, try too hard	Keep trying, slow down
Betrayed	Hurt or revenge	Forgiveness
Worthless	Be self-destructive	Treat yourself well
Fear	Avoidance, Run away	Stay and do what is fearful
Shame	Hide	Be public

Plan For Poise

Make a Plan For Poise to deal with the most upsetting situations that happen in roller derby. What are the situations that make you the angriest or frustrated or other performance-interfering emotion? Below are some things that can make skaters feel upset.

- A teammate says something insulting

- You get feedback from your coach that you don't want to hear

- You get hit really hard

- An opponent calls you a name

- Your coach gives you an instruction you don't want to follow

- An official calls you for something you don't think you did

- You make a mistake during a game

- An opposing skater tells you that you're committing a penalty

Using the Plan For Poise chart, determine how you will remain poised in the face of upsetting thoughts and emotions. Think of some situations that have been problematic for you and come up with a personalized plan to confront, rather than avoid, the uncomfortable thoughts and feelings.

"You have to be less judgmental. Because if you're judgmental you would say 'Why are you doing that,' 'You're supposed to be doing this.''

—Vampire Bunny

Age 11, Skating 4 years

Plan For Poise			
Problem Situation	**Negative Thoughts And Emotions**	**Unhelpful Action**	**Helpful Action**
My teammate gives me advice that I don't want to hear.	*"I wish she would shut up and leave me alone." Frustrated, irritated.*	*Skate off the track and cry or yell at her to stop telling you what to do.*	*Notice I feel irritated, shift my focus to what I need to be doing at the moment. Maybe talk to her after practice.*

Some derby situations make you feel afraid, nervous or worried about experiencing vulnerable emotions such as embarrassment, sadness or disappointment. Consider this situation as an example: A skater is trying out for her league's All-star team. A tryout has all kinds of potential for difficult thoughts and emotions. A skater could be thinking things like, *"I'm not good enough," "I shouldn't be here," "They're going to laugh at me"* and *"I'm going to let my family down."* She might become so overwhelmed with doubts and fears during the tryout that she doesn't skate her best. She may even decide not to try out at all in an attempt to avoid the possibility of thinking and feeling bad. The opposite action (and the one that would take her in the direction of her roller derby goals) would be to face her fears and do the tryout.

The opposite action required to face a fear might seem like too big of a change from a skater's typical actions. If that is the case for you, you can create a ladder that will help you to approach your emotions by slowly climbing to where you want to go in small, achievable steps. What are some activities that the skater in the example above could do to begin to confront her fears? She should start with things that make her feel a little bit afraid but that she thinks she can accomplish.

> "I get a really big adrenaline rush and I get excited. My focus is on the other jammer."
>
> —Ally Oops
>
> Age 17, Skating 4 years

She could start by asking a teammate to watch her go through some of the tryout elements and build from there. The most important thing is when she is feeling fear she must allow herself to simply notice it. She needs to let the feeling coexist with the moment and then refocus on the task at hand. By exposing herself to the emotions she is trying to avoid they will begin to gradually lose their power over her. She will learn that even though she may feel like she is dying, emotions can't actually kill her—it is not truly a life threatening experience. She will learn she can deal with negative thoughts and feelings. She will become poised!

Create your own Face-My-Fear Ladder:

1. Think of a fear-charged roller derby situation that you wish you had handled better.

2. Recall what your action urge was. Looking back, can you see that it took you in the opposite direction from your roller derby goals?

3. What was the action you should have taken instead? Determine what your ultimate goal would be and put that at the top of the Face-My-Fear Ladder Worksheet on the next page.

4. Break down that goal into bitesize steps that can be accomplished little by little to get you where you want to go.

By approaching, rather than avoiding, potentially uncomfortable, difficult or even threatening emotions you will build your ability to tolerate distress and you will move towards your roller derby goals. You are becoming mentally tough!

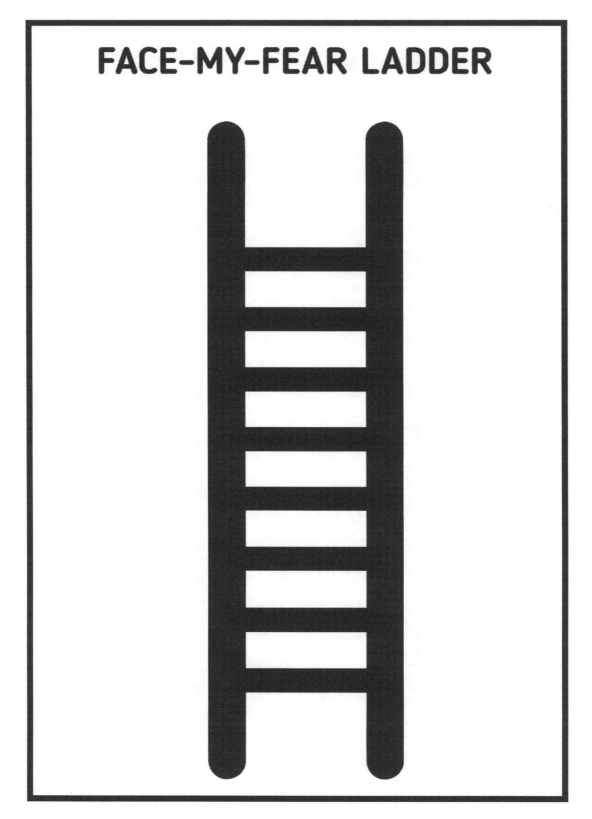

Danny Ngan Photography

Review Committing To Values Exercise

Do you recall the road trip analogy presented earlier in the book? It was about the destination being our roller derby goal and the journey being our values—or how we want to go about achieving our goal. Let's say that you are making a road trip across the country. You have determined where you want to

> "I want to challenge myself and practice more."
>
> —Slim Reaper
>
> Age 16, Skating 7 years

go and what you want the journey to be like. You decided you want the journey to be really Fun (that is your value). What if during the trip your little brother begins pester you in the car? You may start feeling annoyed. Or perhaps you start getting hungry and your parents tell you that it will be another hour until you stop for dinner. You may start to feel frustrated. Would you be able to stay true to your value of having fun? Or would you act on your emotion-of-the-moment? If we allow ourselves to be consumed by our emotions, we will act in ways that are shortsighted and don't keep the bigger picture in perspective. What actions would be necessary to have fun during this trip? It might take keeping a sense of humor, focusing on the scenery outside the car, thinking about how much you really love your little brother, or focusing on your activities in the car such as reading a book or listening to music.

> "Being pushed to the limit and be able to keep myself calm and not let people get to me and focus on what I need to do."
>
> —Kick N Ash
>
> Age 15, Skating 6 years

You have established your roller derby goal and figured out the values you want be aligned with on your way to achieving your goal. Go back and review the values you wrote down on the Committing to Values Exercise in Chapter 7. Are you committed to taking the actions necessary to stay true to these values and achieve your goals? This means accepting that you will experience some emotional bumps in the road along the way.

In-Between Chapters Mindfulness Exercises:

1. Roller derby-related mindful activities for the week: _____

_____

2. Roller derby-related focus training exercise: _____

_____

3. Practice any other mindfulness exercises you have learned daily: _____

_____

You remain poised when experiencing upsetting thoughts and feelings.

What I Have Learned About Myself And My Roller Derby Performance

In each chapter of this book, you are likely to learn a variety of new things about yourself and your derby performance. After you read each chapter, complete this form as soon as possible. The purpose of this is to ensure that you are learning and remembering the important concepts from each chapter.

1._____

_____

_____

2._____

_____

_____

3._____

_____

_____

4._____

_____

_____

5._____

_____

_____

9 PUTTING IT ALL TOGETHER

By now you should be regularly practicing the exercises and taking the actions necessary to promote the skills that are central to optimal roller derby performance:

1. **Mindfulness** to promote self-awareness, task-focused attention, the ability to be in the present moment and shift your focus where it is helpful.

2. **Acceptance** of uncomfortable thoughts and emotions as a normal part of the human experience and a willingness to experience these in order to achieve your roller derby goals and stay true to your values.

3. **Commitment** to the consistent use of the actions necessary to being true to the values you discovered.

The purpose of this chapter is the extend the skills you have developed and encourage the ongoing use of exercises to further improve your roller derby performance. It is important to work on these skills throughout your entire lifetime. The skills of mindfulness, acceptance and commitment will help you in all areas, not just derby. They can help you with school, with relationships, with your job and the pursuit of any sport or hobby.

In this chapter you will also re-take two of the measures that you completed earlier in the book, the Performance Rating Scale and the Mindfulness Attention Awareness Scale. After you have completed them, compare your scores with your previous versions. Hopefully your scores have improved!

ZEN DERBY

By now you have begun to see thoughts and emotions differently than you have in the past. If you are like most people, thoughts and feelings had a lot of power over you and were an important part of your decision making process.

In Zen practice, students strive for the state that you have been working towards with your mindfulness and acceptance exercises. The word "zen" is overused in our society and the meaning has become generalized, but the Upaya Zen Center defines real Zen as "the practice of coming back to the actual right-now-in-this-moment self, coming back to the naturalness, the intimacy and simplicity of our true nature. Zen practice is not about getting away from our life as it is, it is about getting into our life as it is, with all of its vividness, beauty, hardship, joy and sorrow. Zen is a path of awakening: awakening to who we really are, and awakening the aspiration to serve others and take responsibility for all of life."

The bull pictures shown next are a teaching tool created by ancient Zen masters. The images included here were created by a Japanese woodblock print artist named, Tokuriki Tomikichiro. The bull is a representation of our true nature—that which students of Zen are attempting to find and understand. There are ten pictures all together in the series, but these six make good metaphors for the journey your relationship with your thoughts and feelings, or your "self," has taken so far.

"I want to show constant progress. If I was always doing great, how would I know I was doing great?"

—Ginger Slap

Age 15, Skating 4 years

1. Discovering the bull.

2. Catching the bull.

3. Taming the bull.

4. Riding the bull.

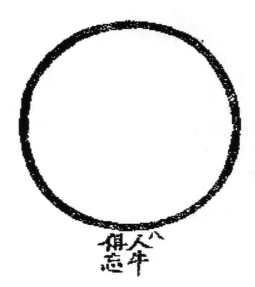

5. The bull transcended.

6. Both bull and self are transcended.

Recomplete The Performance Rating Form

Next recomplete the Performance Rating Form. Progress would be measured by noticing less things have recently got in the way of your performance, higher satisfaction ratings and lower impact ratings.

Performance Rating Form

Please list all of the things that have got in the way of your derby performance (performance barriers) in the last 2 weeks (such as negative thoughts, negative emotions, problems with teammates and lack of concentration):

1. _____

2. _____

3. _____

4. _____

5. _____

0	1	2	3	4	5	6	7	8	9	10
None		**Mild**			**Moderate**		**Strong**		**Extreme**	

Please rate each of the following using the 0 to 10 scale above:

Performance Area	Satisfaction With Performance In This Area (0 to 10)	Impact Of Performance Barrier (0 to 10)
Practice/Training		
Games/Competitions		
Relationships With Coaches		
Relationships with Teammates		
Other (Please describe)		

Focus Training Exercise II

This exercise will help you to further your ability to direct your attention from internal experiences to relevant external elements. You will work on shifting your focus from upsetting thoughts and feelings such as those below to the necessary elements of the actual task at hand. For these exercises you will think of three upsetting derby situations you have been in—one difficult, one challenging and one threatening and follow the directions to train your focus. As a reminder, here are some upsetting thoughts and feelings related to derby:

Thoughts:

How am I doing?

I'm going to mess up.

They are going to laugh at me.

She's better than me.

My coach doesn't like me.

Feelings:

Anxiety

Fear

Anger

Frustration

Embarrassment

Danny Ngan Photography

112

A Difficult Situation

Think of a difficult roller derby performance situation. Try to recall the situation with as many thoughts, feelings and details as possible. Are you feeling the same as if you are back in that moment? Now shift your attention to completing this dot-to-dot activity as fast as possible.

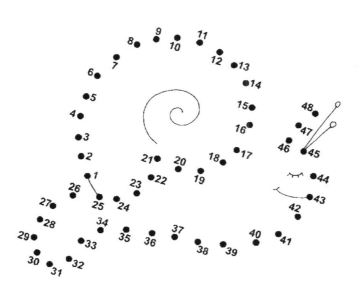

Were you able to shift your attention from being in your head and upset to being in the present moment and focused on the task at hand? In order to be successful at the dot-to-dot activity, what was it necessary for you to focus on? Were your emotions helpful? Were "*what ifs*" or doubts relevant? In order to successfully complete the dot-to-dot task it is only necessary to focus on finding the next number.

Think about the difficult roller derby performance situation you were thinking about. Ask yourself these three questions about that situation:

1. What was the roller derby task and how can you tell if you've done it well? This is an exercise in self-awareness. Figure out what you were trying to accomplish.

2. Where has your attention usually been focused during these situations? Typically, for problematic situations, our attention becomes too focused on what is going on inside our head.

3. Where should your attention be focused during the task? Determine what is relevant to focus on in order for you to do this task well.

A Challenging Situation

Now think of a challenging roller derby situation. Again, try to recall the situation as vividly as you can. As soon as you are feeling the same emotions and thinking the same thoughts as you were that day, shift your attention to completing the dot-to-dot activity below as fast as possible.

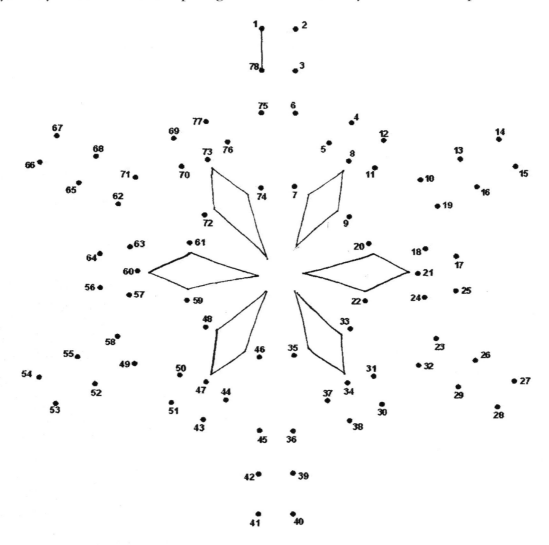

Evaluate how well you were able to shift your attention from negative thoughts and feelings to being fully present and engaged in this task. What were you aware of during the task? What were you thinking and feeling? Now ask yourself the same three questions about the challenging derby situation:

1. What was the roller derby task and how can you tell if you've done it well?
2. Where has your attention usually been focused during these situations?
3. Where should your attention be focused during the task?

A Threatening Situation

Last think of a roller derby performance situation that felt threatening. Use all of your senses to immerse yourself in that situation. What were you thinking about? What emotions were you experiencing? Now complete dot-to-dot activity on the next page as quickly as you can.

Eric Lyons Photography

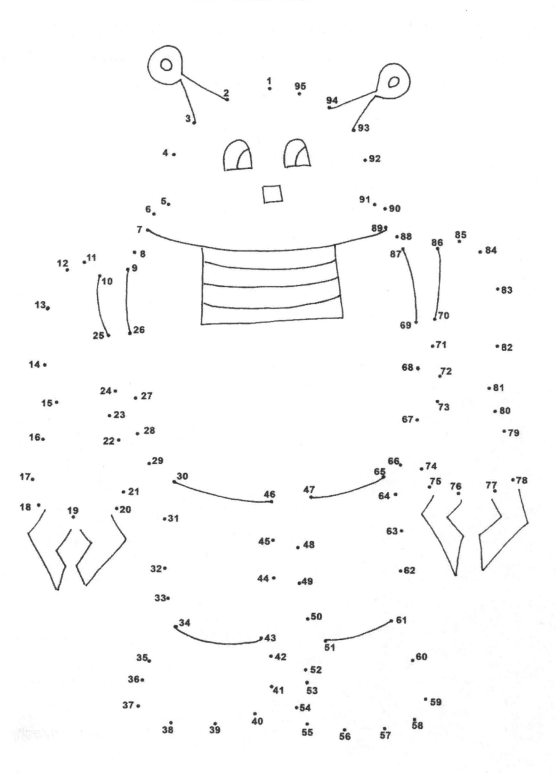

When you are finished, check in with yourself. How easily you were able shift your attention from the thoughts and feelings related to the threatening situation to the task at hand. What was this exercise like for you? Finally, ask yourself the three questions below:

1. What was the roller derby task and how can you tell if you've done it well?
2. Where has your attention usually been focused during these situations?
3. Where should your attention be focused during the task?

This activity can also be done using the 1 To 100 Number Grid on the next page. To use the grid, try to find a consecutive sequence of ten numbers (e.g. from 40 to 49) as quickly as you can. Find a different sequence of ten each time or you can count by twos, threes, etc. All focus training exercises teach you that even when you are stressed or upset you can shift your attention to what is necessary to do your best and hold it there.

Derby isn't all sunny skies. Sometimes you have to deal with some storms—this is a hardcore, challenging sport. You won't always feel good on your way to success. But when the happy moments come, bask in their glow completely.

84	27	51	78	59	52	13	85	61	55
28	60	92	4	97	90	31	57	29	33
32	96	65	39	80	77	49	86	18	70
76	87	71	95	98	81	1	46	88	100
48	82	89	47	35	17	10	42	62	34
44	67	93	11	7	43	72	94	69	56
53	79	5	22	54	74	58	14	91	2
6	68	99	75	26	15	41	66	20	40
50	9	64	8	38	30	36	45	83	24
3	73	21	23	16	37	25	19	12	63

1 To 100 Number Grid

Focus Training Exercise III

This exercise will take your ability to pay attention to the task at hand to the next level. To be mentally tough it is necessary to be able to focus on what is needed to get the job done no matter how tough the job.

Think about a roller derby performance situation that caused you to experience very strong negative emotions such as anger, anxiety, fear or worry. Put yourself back in that situation. Where do you feel the emotions in your body? What were you thinking about? Once you are having the same thoughts and feelings you were at that time complete this task:

1. Think of an anger, anxiety, fear or worry-provoking roller derby situation.
2. Stand up and balance on one foot for 30 seconds.
3. Try to be as steady as possible.

After the 30 seconds have passed, reflect on what it was important for you to focus on in order to do this task successfully. Were you able to shift your attention from upsetting thoughts and feelings to what was relevant to completing the task at hand? What is relevant to focus on in order to be able to complete this task successfully? Most people find it important to concentrate on something on the floor or in front of them, to notice how their weight is distributed over the foot they are balancing on and to keep it even, to keep a slight bend in the balancing leg, to keep the body as still as possible and to pay attention to the breath, making sure it is calm and not too rapid.

"Learning is important to me. Getting to know more things is what I like to do, go outside my box and learn new things."

—Tap Out

Age 13, Skating 3 ½ years

Did you notice any negative thoughts and feelings returning during this exercise? If so, were you able to gently shift your focus back to the present moment and the task?

Next you are going to repeat this activity except this time you are going to pretend that you are at the center of a tree branch that stretches out high above a river. The tree branch is 40 feet above the river.

1. Pretend you are on a tree branch balancing high above a river.

2. Stand up, close your eyes and balance on one foot for 30 seconds.

3. Try to be as steady as possible.

Evaluate any changes in your ability to easily shift your focus between your internal experiences to the task at hand. Was it more difficult to do as the stakes for the task went up? How well do you think you could do this if you really were standing on a tree branch high above a river? Would your thoughts and fears overwhelm you? Or would you be able to get out of your head and focus on what you needed to do to be successful?

Last, you are going to repeat all of the above adding jumping jacks to make you feel some of the bodily sensations (faster heart rate) that come along with feeling anxious.

1. Do 10 jumping jacks.

2. Pretend you are on a tree branch balancing high above a river

3. Balance on one foot for 30 seconds.

4. Try to be as steady as possible.

How did you do that time? Jumping jacks increase your heart rate which can trigger the mind-body stress feedback loop (you will read more about this in Chapter 10) by sending messages to the brain that something is wrong. In order to be successful at this task you have to be able to tolerate distressing physical sensations that often go along with feeling negative thoughts and feelings and still be able to shift your focus away from them to what is relevant to successfully completing the task at hand.

"Derby has changed my life. I wouldn't be who I am today without it. Cherish every moment you have with your team and everything you do. Your team is more than a team. They become family. Also cherish every moment, because sooner or later it'll all be over."

—Annihilate-Her

Age 18, Skating 4 years

Heart Full Of Values

By this point in the book you should be pretty firm on what your roller derby goals and values are. You should also know what actions you need to commit to in order to stay true to your values. Fill in the Heart Full Of Values worksheet on the next page, writing your values at the heart center, your value-driven actions in the middle circle, and your roller derby goals in the outer circle.

My goals are what I want to achieve in this sport.

My values tell me why my goals are important to me.

My value-driven actions are how I am going to stay true

to my values while I achieve my goals.

Danny Ngan Photography

Heart Full Of Values Worksheet

Retake The Mindfulness Attention Awareness Scale

Mindful Attention Awareness Scale (MAAS) Day-to-Day Experiences

Instructions: Below is a collection of statements about your everyday experience. Using the 1-6 scale below, please indicate how frequently or infrequently you currently have each experience. Please answer according to what really reflects your experience rather than what you think your experience should be. Please treat each item separately from every other item.

1	2	3	4	5	6
Always	Frequently	Somewhat frequently	Somewhat infrequently	Infrequently	Never

I could be experiencing some emotion and not be conscious of it until sometime later.

1   2   3   4   5   6

I break or spill things because of carelessness, not paying attention, or thinking of something else.

1   2   3   4   5   6

I find it difficult to stay focused on what's happening in the present.

1   2   3   4   5   6

I tend to walk quickly to get where I'm going without paying attention to what I experience along the way.

1   2   3   4   5   6

I tend not to notice feelings of physical tension or discomfort until they really grab my attention.

1   2   3   4   5   6

I forget a person's name almost as soon as I've been told it for the first time.

1   2   3   4   5   6

It seems I am "running on automatic," without much awareness of what I'm doing.

1   2   3   4   5   6

I rush through activities without being really attentive to them.

           1   2   3   4   5   6

I get so focused on the goal I want to achieve that I lose touch with what I'm doing right now to get there.

           1   2   3   4   5   6

I do jobs or tasks automatically, without being aware of what I'm doing.

           1   2   3   4   5   6

I find myself listening to someone with one ear, doing something else at the same time.

           1   2   3   4   5   6

I go places on 'automatic pilot' and then wonder why I went there.

           1   2   3   4   5   6

I find myself preoccupied with the future or the past.

           1   2   3   4   5   6

I find myself doing things without paying attention.

           1   2   3   4   5   6

I snack without being aware that I'm eating.

           1   2   3   4   5   6

Scoring: To score the MAAS scale, simply compute an average of the 15 items. Higher scores reflect higher levels of mindfulness.

Commitment to Values

The end of these 7 chapters on the MAC approach to mental toughness marks the beginning of a lifelong journey of self-awareness, acceptance of the ongoing difficulties that are part of life and a commitment to those actions that are most meaningful to you, both inside and outside of roller derby.

Commitment To Values Form

I commit to taking the actions necessary to stay true to my chosen values on the way to achieving my roller derby goals. I accept that I may not always be feeling or thinking in a way that feels good, but I know I can still focus my attention on what is relevant to get the job done.

Signature/Date: X_____

Yoga For Flexibility

Seated Twist. A flexible mind and an inflexible spine don't go together. Can what is twisted always be untwisted? Ideas that are held stubbornly will make untwisting harder because of pride. This book has many concepts that may have been new for you. It takes flexibility to be give up old ways of doing things and try something different.

Start sitting on the floor with your legs straight out in front of you. Bend your knees, put your feet on the floor, and then slide your left foot under your right leg to the outside of your right hip. Lay the outside of the left leg on the floor. Step the right foot over the left leg and stand it on the floor outside your left hip. The right knee will point directly at the sky. Exhale and twist towards the inside of the right thigh. Press the right hand against the floor behind you and set your left hand on your left foot. Let the twisting come from your core rather than trying to force the twist by pulling or pushing with your arms. Lift and lengthen your torso. Look over your right shoulder if it feels comfortable. Relax into the pose, rather than holding it rigidly. With every inhalation lift a little more, with every exhalation twist a little more. Hold for three to five breaths, release back to your starting point on an exhalation and repeat on the other side.

"I want to be remembered as the person that is not afraid to get down and dirty but off the track I'm one of the nicest people you could meet and a really cool person to hang out with."

—Irene Yonek

Age 14, Skating 5 years

While you hold this pose reflect on the followings:

1. How flexible do I want to be in changing old ways?
2. Is there anything I need to undo?
3. Think of times when a twist of events turned out for the best?

My Post-Book Practice Plan

Your Post-Book Practice Plan is where you can write down all the things you will continue to work on after you are done reading this book. You can write down your favorite mindfulness exercises, roller derby-relevant mindfulness exercises and focus training exercises. By combining your Post-Book

> "I find jamming really fun because you get to go your fastest."
>
> —Lucky Harms
>
> Age 13, Skating 4 years

Practice Plan with your Goal Mapping Templates, Heart Full Of Values Worksheet and Commitment To Values Form there is little that will get in the way of you continuing your journey towards mental toughness. Mental toughness is a direction, not a destination—you must keep working on these skills throughout your whole life.

Look at these every day:

1. Goal Mapping Templates
2. Heart Full Of Values Worksheet
3. Commitment To Values Form
4. My Post-Book Practice Plan

Danny Ngan Photography

My Post-Book Practice Plan

Basic Mindfulness Practice:

Exercise	Situation	Frequency

Roller Derby-Related Mindfulness Practice:

Exercise	Situation	Frequency

Roller Derby-Related Focus Training Exercises:

Exercise	Situation	Frequency

You will be mindful of your thoughts and feelings,

staying focused on what you need to do to be successful.

You are committed to doing what it takes to stay true to your values.

This is the best way to achieve your goals.

What I Have Learned About Myself And My Roller Derby Performance

In each chapter of this book, you are likely to learn a variety of new things about yourself and your derby performance. After you read each chapter, complete this form as soon as possible. The purpose of this is to ensure that you are learning and remembering the important concepts from each chapter.

1._____

_____

_____

2._____

_____

_____

3._____

_____

_____

4._____

_____

_____

5._____

_____

_____

10 CONFIDENCE

Confidence the belief that you can succeed. Confidence is connected to the concept of self-esteem—the value you see yourself having in the world. Confidence and self-esteem are related but different. If a person has high self-esteem they are more likely to be a confident person, but not always. If you have high self-esteem, you are probably going to feel pretty good about yourself in all areas of your life. However, you can have confidence in certain areas of your life and not others. For example, you can be super

> "I'm always trying to improve myself which is a very self-esteem thing for me, that I can just get something down."
>
> —Blackheart Blockher
>
> Age 14, Skating 4 years

confident in derby but not at dancing or getting up and speaking in front of the class.

Self-esteem can be difficult to build because simply telling yourself or being told that you are a winner may not be enough to make you truly believe you are. The advantage of confidence is that it is solidly built on your achievements. Confidence builds when you take action and try things you find hard—when you go outside your comfort zone. This chapter will help you to increase your self-esteem *and* your confidence so you can go out and be who you want to be and accomplish the things you want to accomplish. Confidence is all about action and action will get you results. The confidence boosting activities in this chapter will help you to be able to take the actions necessary to fulfill your dreams— roller derby and otherwise.

Confidence is all about action.

Since past accomplishments give you confidence to keep moving forward, what gave you the confidence to accomplish those things in the first place? Some say that we are born with confidence and it isn't until we have some bad experiences that it dwindles. Some say we develop confidence as we experience successes. Whether we are born confident or it develops as we go, here are some other elements that influence our belief that we can succeed:

- Seeing other skaters performing a skill
- Feeling healthy
- Trusting your teammates and coaches
- Having the support of your family
- A practice environment where it feels safe to make mistakes

Lack of confidence comes from one place—fear. When we allow ourselves to be driven by our fears we lose control over our ability to achieve our goals.

- Fear about what people will think of you
- Fear of failure
- Fear of success
- Fear of injury

What came first? The action that built the confidence or the confidence to take the action?

Pride

Sometimes it is difficult for us to talk about accomplishments that we are proud of. We may feel like we are bragging or being conceited. Yet, when we acknowledge what we've been able to do in the past, it will build our confidence to tackle things in the future because we know that we can overcome obstacles, work hard, and meet challenges.

Complete the statement below with as many examples as you can think of. They don't need to all be roller derby examples. When we recognize what we have been able to accomplish in one area of life we can use that knowledge to give us the confidence we need to tackle another area.

"I am proud that I…"

1.

2.

3.

4.

5.

Cory Lund Photography

Confidence Blueprint

Draw a picture of the new confident you. How will you appear? What will others see? What kinds of things will you be saying? What kinds of things will you be doing?

A Confident Me!

Visualize Confidence

Below is a guided visualization adapted from a meditation in Marneta Viegas' book, *Aladdin's Magic Carpet*. It will help you to focus on the confidence inside of you. Have somebody read it to you while you relax in a comfortable position.

Close your eyes and be very still. Imagine that you are Mary Poppins and you can fly. Pick up your magic flying umbrella, open it and hold it up in the air. Close your fingers on the comfortable handle of the magic

"I push myself really hard and I make goals like if someone on the team is better than me I say 'wow I'm envious" and try to get to their level."

—Ally Oops

Age 17, Skating 4 years

umbrella and let the wind take you up into the air. Just allow yourself to hang freely from the umbrella. As you dangle in the air, allow your body to totally relax. Let your feet relax as they sway gently in the air and let your legs hang. Let all the tension melt away in your legs as you enjoy this feeling of floating in the air. Let your arms and shoulders be relaxed. Enjoy the wind brushing against your face, relaxing your eyes, your ears, your forehead, your cheeks, your mouth. You feel as free as a bird. If your mind begins to wander and you find yourself thinking about something other than flying, simply notice and gently bring it back.

Inside you feel so confident. The more confident you feel, the higher you can fly. You are so light and airborne that your arms will never feel tired. Sometimes the wind changes direction and you start to pick up speed and fly faster. It feels so exhilarating to be rushing and swooshing through the sky. Sometimes, the wind dips and you drift down until it picks up again and sends you

riding through the air at a brisk pace. Other times, the wind drops and turns to a light breeze, allowing you to float gently through the sky. It feels as if you are walking on air.

Keep flying in the air for as long as you wish.

And now when you are ready wiggle your fingers and toes, have a big stretch and open your eyes.

"Mom is an inspiration. She's been skating for the same amount of time and she pushes me to get better. She's a role model for me."

—Kick N Ash

Age 15, Skating 6 years

The Mind-Body Stress Feedback Loop

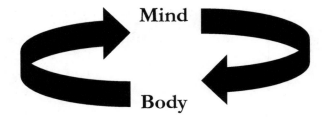

The mind-body stress feedback loop is a system for keeping you safe in times of danger. Signals travel from your mind, to your body, and then back to your mind. The loop continues as long as the mind is perceiving a threat. This becomes tricky when the mind can't tell the difference between emotional threats and physical ones. Your mind can perceive many things as a threat such as critical game situations, trying something new at practice and going in front of a big crowd to accept an MVP award. This can cause problems for your confidence when you respond to the body's physiological responses to fear and anxiety as if there is actual danger. This would make you want to stay in your comfort zone. It is up to you to listen to your mind and body and make a decision whether or not to take a chance. If you decide to go for it then you will need to tolerate the physiological sensations and turn your focus to what is needed for the task at hand. Physiological responses to stress mean your body and mind are on alert—you are ready for roller derby! (If you're really unsure if you're ready for something always check with your coach or parent.)

This is how the mind-body stress feedback loop can work:

1.   Mind: Your mind perceives a threat. You feel fear and anxiety.

2.   Body: Your heart starts to race.

3.   Mind: Your mind notices your heart is racing and tells itself, "Yep that's what I thought, we're in danger." The idea that you are in danger and your body needs to prepare to protect you is reinforced.

Stretch Out Of Your Comfort Zone

Don't let your comfort zone become your prison. Write down one small task that you can do tomorrow which will slightly stretch you out of your comfort zone. It could be volunteering for something at practice, asking the coach a question, talking to somebody you don't know very well or anything else that you've been afraid or uncomfortable to do. Once you've accomplished this task you will be out of your former comfort zone and a step closer to being the skater you want to be. Nothing can hold you back!

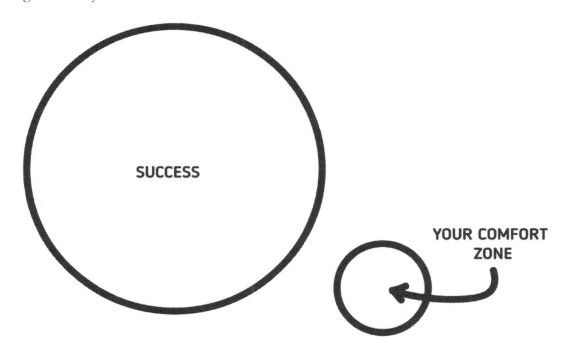

Put Your Roller Derby Name Into Action

Write down your derby name and think of a positive, action-oriented word for each letter. Select words that you identify with, want to be and that you can translate into actions. A few ideas for each letter of the alphabet are below. Come up with your own ideas as well! What can you do and say each day to *be* these words?

> "Roller derby is my life. I skate Mondays, Tuesdays, Wednesdays, Thursdays, Saturdays and Sundays. I do roller derby because I love it."
>
> —Slim Reaper
>
> Age 16, Skating 7 years

An alphabet of action and positivity:

A Assertive, Authentic, Attentive

B Balanced, Blissful

C Calm, Consistent, Cheerful

D Devoted, Disciplined, Dependable

E Enthusiastic, Excited, Energetic

F Fearless, Focused, Forgiving

G Generous, Grateful, Giggly

H Happy, Helpful, Humble, Honest

I Inspirational, Invincible, Involved

J Joyous, Just, Joker

K Kind, Knowledgeable, Killer

L Loving, Loyal, Leader

M Majestic, Mellow, Motivational

N Nurturing, Nice

O Optimistic, Open, Original

P Positive, Proud, Powerful

Q Quiet, Quality, Quick

R Relaxed, Resilient

S Spontaneous, Sweet, Supercharged

T Trusting, Tolerant, Triumphant

U Unique, Understanding

V Valuable, Virtuous, Vibrant

W Worthy, Wondrous, Wise

X Xenial, X-ray Visionary

Y Youthful, Yearner

Z Zany, Zippy, Zealous

Be...

Yoga For Your Best Self

As mentioned, our bodies and our minds are connected. When we are thinking defeating thoughts it will be reflected in defeated body language. We may hang our heads or take short, half-hearted steps. When we are thinking confidently we hold our heads up and take long, self-assured strides. The flip side of this is when we act confident it is reflected in our thinking in confident ways. It is not easy to control our thoughts but we can work to have control over our bodies.

> "Literally everything I do is for derby. I hydrate for derby. Everything I eat is for derby. I practice 4 days a week and go to every scrimmage. Everything I do is for derby."
>
> —Ginger Slap
>
> Age 15, Skating 4 years

Here is a confidence boosting yoga pose:

Half-Moon Pose. This pose can be challenging for a mind full of self-doubt. On the flip side, it can quickly build confidence. You can move straight into Half-Moon pose from Warrior II pose. From Warrior II, keep your left leg bent, reach your left hand to touch the ground about twelve inches beyond the little toe of your left foot. Press firmly into the four corners of the left foot, using the left hand to help 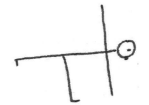 you balance, slowly lift the right leg until it is parallel (or a little above parallel) to the floor. Keep the right leg straight and strong, reaching through the heel. Straighten your left leg but keep a slight bend. Rotate your upper body so that you are open, facing out. Reach your right arm straight up so that it is stacked over your left arm. You can face your gaze anywhere that feels comfortable— down, out or up. Hold for three to five breaths and then slowly come out of it, with control, back into Warrior II. Repeat on other side.

It can be challenging to feel confident if you're feeling really wobbly. Explore the more difficult poses playfully, with a sense of humor. Don't take yourself too seriously. Don't be worried about looking silly or being imperfect. Don't be afraid to take chances. Don't be overly concerned about how others will judge you. Taking this approach to practicing yoga will directly translate into the confidence you need to go after your goals in derby.

A Confident Core

Yoga poses also boost confidence by strengthening your core. Most people think the core is just about the abs, but your core muscle group is made up from lots of different parts of your body. Sure, your core is made up from the muscles in the front of your body that run from just below your sternum to your waist. Also part of the core muscle group is your lower back and outer-middle back muscles and the muscles

> "I feel like this is my sport. I kind of fit in here. I would do other sports but I feel like this is mine."
>
> —Lucky Harms
>
> Age 13, Skating 4 years

running along your sides from your ribs to your upper hips. Some people are surprised to learn that leg muscles including the hips, hamstrings and even the glutes are considered part of the core muscle group. A strong core is important to the physical aspects of playing roller derby in all sorts of ways—and being strong, stable and balanced gives you confidence that you can get out there and do what you need to do. A solid core also gives you confidence beyond that. When you feel strong on the inside, you can start to trust your body's inner wisdom and you stop second guessing yourself. Your inner strength becomes translated into outer strength that you can direct into personal power on and off the track. A strong core equals a confident you!

Here are three yoga poses that are great for strengthening the core muscles. You can connect them, doing them in a sequence, to create a flow. As with all yoga practice, don't hold your breath—remember to breathe!

Plank Pose. Come to all fours, with knees several inches behind hips. Point fingers straight ahead and spread them like rays of the sun. Press down through the four corners of each hand.

> "I kind of just think about the good parts. So if I think we have a bad wall I will be the person to fix it."
>
> —Tap Out
>
> Age 13, Skating 3 ½ years

Straighten one leg back, turn toes under, and place foot on floor. Do the same with the other leg and come into a push up position with your shoulders directly over or slightly behind wrists. Lift your legs, hips, belly and head until body is straight like a board. Your tailbone is kept tucked toward the floor. Press out through your heels and top of head. To avoid sagging at the hips and belly, breathe into your low back and imagine it lifting up like a balloon. Hold for two breaths.

Downward Dog. From plank pose, exhale and press down through the hands and feet. Lift your hips up and back, lifting your tailbone towards the sky. Relax your head and neck, looking back towards your knees and press  your heels towards the earth. Now you are in downward dog pose. Hold for two breaths before flowing into the next pose.

 **Crescent Lunge.** From downward dog, inhale and bring your right foot forward, between the hands by the right thumb. Stay on the ball of the back foot and raise your upper body towards the sky. Keep your shoulders over your hips and your knee over your ankle. Reach both arms up, activating through the fingers. You can look up towards your hands or straight ahead, whichever feels the most comfortable. Hold for two breaths. Bring your hands to the floor in front of you, step back into plank, push up into downward dog and repeat on the other side.

You are confident. Go out there and be amazing!

What I Have Learned About Myself And My Roller Derby Performance

In each chapter of this book, you are likely to learn a variety of new things about yourself and your derby performance. After you read each chapter, complete this form as soon as possible. The purpose of this is to ensure that you are learning and remembering the important concepts from each chapter.

1._____

_____

_____

2._____

_____

_____

3._____

_____

_____

4._____

_____

_____

5._____

_____

_____

11 THE SCIENCE OF TEAMBUILDING

Teambuilding, or teamwork, is such an important subject in roller derby it gets two chapters in this book. Chapter 11 teaches you the science behind teambuilding. You will learn about sportsmanship (sports-person-ship), communication, team cultures, brain-based coping and emotional honesty. Chapter 12 is more hands-on where you will get to do lots of fun teambuilding activities.

When skaters are asked to identify what is important or valuable to them about roller derby, many say it is their team or teammates. However, one of the best parts about derby can also be one of the most difficult parts. Conflict with others, or "drama," is one of the most common complaints skaters have about this sport. It is the top reason given for bad behavior and derby-related stress—and often the reason skaters quit altogether. It takes an incredible amount of mental toughness to maintain poise in the face of drama:

- to be able to respond instead of react
- to act according to values rather than emotions

> "NO DRAMA. Stupid drama is the worst. Just remember that even though this is a sport, have fun. Remember that these people will have your back till the end."
>
> —Annihilate-Her
>
> Age 18, Skating 4 years

If one of the things you value about roller derby is your teammates, then you must show this by your actions. Here are some things that could get in the way of a skater valuing their teammates:

- Talking behind people's backs

- Jealousy

- Holding grudges

- Only hanging around with certain people

- Lying

- Judging people

Here are some things a skater could do more of or change in order to value their teammates:

- Trying to get to know everyone on the team

- Being happy for others when they do well

- Talking more to all skaters on the team

- Being more social

What are some things that could get in the way of you valuing your team?

1.

2.

3.

What do you need to do more of or change in order to value your team?

1.

2.

3.

Seek first to understand.

Sportsmanship (Sports-person-ship)

The Junior Roller Derby Association's (JRDA) Code of Conduct says, "Skaters will lead by example and demonstrate good sportsmanship with fellow skaters, coaches, officials, parents, and other attendees at every game and practice." Sportsmanship or good sporting behavior is what we believe is the right way and wrong way to act in sports. It has to do with treating yourself and others with dignity, respect and fairness. Being a good sport means if winning and fairness come into conflict, fairness will come first. Sportsmanship is related to teamwork because how you act affects everyone around you. Below are

"Some of us misunderstand stuff and then it goes from one person to another and when it finally gets to the actually person it isn't even how it started and it causes a big team argument. It caused a loss. We were so mad at each other we didn't want to work with each other.

—The Crusher

Age 16, Skating 6 years

three true stories of sportsmanship from Sports Illustrated Kids and Buzzfeed.com to inspire you!

1. "High school rowers, James Konopka and Nick Mead were well on their way to medaling in a race when one of the opposing boats capsized. As this was the Philadelphia area in November with temperatures only reaching about 45 degrees, Konopka and Mead decided to abandon their medal hopes and help their opponents out of the freezing water. After the two fallen rowers were out of the water, the heroes decided that they still should finish the race. So they did."

2. "Meghan Vogel of West Liberty-Salem High School track team was in last place of the finals when the runner ahead of her, Arden McMath began to collapse. Rather than continuing past McMath and avoid a last place finish, Vogel stopped, picked up her injured competitor and carried her the final 20 meters of the race and then across the finish line. Ahead of herself."

3. "It was the first game of a double header with two outs and runners on first and second in the 7th inning. Senior pitcher for Florida, Chelsea Oglevie, was only one strike away from ending the game and getting the win in the final appearance of her career when Kara Oberer stepped up to the plate. Rather, she limped towards the batter's box. Despite a bad knee, Oberer told her coach she could bat, knowing a base hit would put the game in her team's favor. On her second swing, Oberer crushed the ball over the left field fence—a three-

run homer that gave their team a 4-2 lead. As she was running the bases, however, her knee locked up and she could not take another step. Florida's second baseman Leah Pemberton ran to help, and Chelsea Oglevie joined. The two carried their stunned foe around the bases."

Think about situations in roller derby where you have witnessed good sportsmanship. How can you be a good sport? Here are some examples:

- Helping up a downed skater—even if they aren't hurt.
- Loaning equipment to an opponent if they need something.
- Cheering for great plays by your opponents.
- Refusing to take advantage of injured opponents.
- Respecting your captains and coaches.
- Playing by the rules—earn your win!
- Bringing your A game—it shows your opponents they are worthy of your best!
- Not blaming others for your mistakes.
- Taking responsibility if you behave badly.
- Thanking the officials after a game.

Can you think of some more ways you can show sportsmanship?

- _____
- _____

Be fierce and friendly.

Communication

There are two different types of communication—verbal and nonverbal. Verbal communication uses sounds and words to get our message across. Nonverbal communication uses things like our gestures, body language and facial expressions to help us convey our message. 90% of our communication is non-verbal.

All types of communication can be categorized into basic necessary parts—a sender, a receiver and a message. Even though this seems simple, there are many ways that communication can break down and misunderstandings occur.

Sender   Message   Receiver

The message that the sender wants to communicate goes through a process of *coding*, or putting it into verbal, written and/or nonverbal language. In order to understand the message, the receiver has to *decode* it—interpreting the words, facial expressions, body language, etc. The codes we know are based on what we have learned during our life experiences. Codes vary between cultures, geographical areas, families and even between groups of friends. Think about private jokes, slang or certain forms of sarcasm that others outside of your group may not understand.

"Sometimes you hate them for the moment but then you're going to have to see them the next Wednesday and the next Sunday. Sometimes you feel like you want to hurt them, to wipe them out."

—Slim Reaper

Age 16, Skating 7 years

All communication problems are two-person problems. This means misunderstandings are the fault of *both* the sender and the receiver. Think about how you would code a message to three different people: a 4-year-old, someone who speaks a different language and your best friend. It is important for the sender to choose the best way to code a message so that the receiver can understand.

Common receiving problems include not really listening so that you miss important information, not having the knowledge to understand the message and adding our own meaning that was not really intended by the sender. Communication has been effective when the receiver understands what the sender meant to convey.

Consider this scenario during a practice:

Skater B is a jammer and was struggling to get through the pack during a jam. When she comes off the track, Skater A makes a comment to her.

Skater A: "You should try skating up the middle instead of going to the outside."

Skater B: Thinks Skater A is criticizing her, feels hurt and angry, skates away and cries.

What was the message that Skater A intended? What was the message that Skater B received? If Skater A's intention is to help Skater B out so that she can be a successful jammer, then Skater B could have been better job at decoding the message to realize Skater A meant no harm and not taken offense. Skater A could have been more sensitive to the fact that Skater B is down on herself about her jamming and just offered encouragement like, "You kept fighting!" rather than give advice. The situation, and the messages that were sent and received, can change based on a number of variables. What if the skaters were best friends? What if the skaters were sisters? What if the skaters did not like each other? The critical piece of information here is no single person is 100% at fault for communication problems. Both people involved must take responsibility for effective communication.

Cory Lund Photography

Types Of Nonverbal Communication

Facial expressions. The facial expressions for happiness, sadness, anger, contempt, surprise, fear and disgust are the same across cultures. Eye rolling, smirks and head shakes are very visually apparent ways to communicate lots of mean, judgmental things including disrespect, disgust and irritation. Be sure your nonverbal messages are aligned with the person you want to be.

Body movements and posture. This category includes all of the communication we do with our body. Leaning in towards a person shows interest. Turning away from a person can show dislike. Standing tall demonstrates confidence while slouching can show laziness or not taking things seriously. Crossing arms or legs may show defensiveness or not being open to communicating. Presenting open palms can show honesty and openness.

Gestures. These are ways we communicate with our hands. Pointing, waving, palm-to-face, beckoning, clenching your fist, the peace sign, the OK sign, the middle finger…unlike the seven facial expressions mentioned above, gestures and other nonverbal forms of communication vary across cultures.

Eye contact. The way you look at someone can communicate many things including hostility, affection or understanding. Direct eye contact can show confidence while looking to the side can show irritation. Looking up can indicate thinking about something or boredom. Looking down can show shyness, shame, or respect. Lack of eye contact may indicate being uninterested, ashamed of something or that something is difficult to talk about.

Touch. Touch can be affectionate, encouraging, degrading or reassuring depending it on the type. Touch includes hugs, patting someone's head, grasping someone's arm, and slapping someone's back.

Space. How closely you stand next to someone can show affection, aggression or dominance. Most people feel uncomfortable if anyone other than someone they are super close with enters into their personal space bubble.

Voice. The way we say something is as important as our actual words. This includes how fast or slow we speak, how loudly or softly we speak and our tone. Talking louder or more aggressively may show a person is not feeling heard or understood. To illustrate the importance of tone and volume, try saying the word, "Thanks," in a way that conveys more than one meaning—one nice and one not so nice.

Use the 7 C's to improve your communication:

1. **Clear.** Don't beat around the bush and don't wander off topic. Say what you mean instead of only hinting at it.

2. **Consistent.** For your communication to be effective, you've got to make sure that your message is the same from day to day and from person to person.

3. **Credible.** Speak the truth. It's not easy to build trust, and once you've lost it, it may be gone forever.

4. **Confident**. Be confident in what you are saying. Know what you are talking about. If you believe in what you are saying, people will believe in you.

5. **Civil.** You really don't need to beat people up or make people feel stupid when you communicate. Use polite words and don't shout.

6. **Concise.** Cut to the chase when communicating. Think about what it is you really want the other person to understand and focus on that message.

7. **Compassionate.** Be considerate (which is another C!) of the feelings of others, and be kind when you communicate. Instead of tearing people down, take the opportunity to build them up. People will be more open to hearing what you have to say when they aren't busy being protective of their feelings.

Problem Solving

What is drama? Drama is when situations that have a fairly easy solution are dealt with in negative ways such as backstabbing, gossiping, and lying. Drama is the most common complaint skaters have about derby. In this section you will learn some positive steps you can take to deal with problems with your teammates when you have them.

The Problem Solving Wheel can help you to remember you have choices when you are upset. Always start with the S.T.I.C. acronym (Himelstein, Center for Adolescent Studies) and go from there.

S.T.I.C. means:

Stop. Respond instead of reacting to your emotions.

Take a breath. Create space between your emotion and your action.

Imagine. Use your mindfulness skills to observe your thoughts and feelings without judgment.

Choose. Decide how you want to respond—stay aligned with your values.

Danny Ngan Photography

Problem Solving Wheel

If you decide the problem needs to be talked out with the others involved, you can use the Steps to Conflict Resolution from Safeyouth.org below. Get your coach or parents to help mediate if necessary.

Steps To Conflict Resolution:

1. **Set the Stage.** Agree to try to work together to find a solution peacefully. Establish the ground rules—there will be no name calling, blaming, sarcasm, shouting or interrupting.

2. **Gather perspectives.** Each skater describes the dispute from his or her perspective, without interruption. Listeners pay close attention and then ask questions in a non-threatening manner to make sure they understand. Listeners considers not only what the other skater wants but why they want it.

3. **Find common values.** Figure out which facts or issues all skaters agree on and why different issues are important to each person. What do you have in common? It may be as simple as a mutual desire to do what is best for the team.

4. **Create options.** Brainstorm about possible solutions to the problem. Come up with a list of options without immediately judging them or feeling committed to them. Try to think of solutions where both skaters gain something—think win-win! Be creative and come up with a solution that all involved feel good about, where both walk away feeling their needs were met.

5. **Evaluate options.** After a number of options are suggested, each skater will discuss his or her thoughts about each. Skaters will then negotiate and will often need to compromise in order to reach a conclusion that is acceptable to both. They may need to agree to disagree about some issues to reach an understanding.

6. **Create an agreement.** Skaters involved will clearly state their agreement and may even want to write it down. If necessary, they set up a time to check back to see how the agreement is working.

If you use an approach like this to resolve problems, you will find that conflicts don't have to be avoided and they don't need to lead to drama. A lot of social problems can be solved simply by making an effort to help the other person feel heard and understood.

Don't insult your gender by accepting drama as something that has to happen when large groups of females spend a lot of time together.

The Brain Team

According to Paul MacLean, we have three distinct brains that evolved over time and now all live together inside our skull—the reptilian, the limbic and the neocortex. The three parts of the brain work together and influence one another. The Brain Works Project says these three parts can be considered our "Brain Team." Each member of our brain team plays a role in how we cope with upsets.

The reptilian brain is the oldest of the three parts of our brain. This part of the brain is in charge of our defenses and makes sure we protect ourselves so we survive. The reptilian brain senses both emotional upsets and physical upsets and responds the same way for each. This part of our brain then sends us danger signals that alert the other parts of our brain. If the limbic and neocortex don't understand this part of the brain and decide what the right course of action is, we can find ourselves always acting if we are in physical danger.

These are some of the jobs of the reptilian brain:

1. Protection from threats

2. Attack or hide reactions

3. Aggression

4. Anger

5. Fear

6. Revenge

7. Territorial behavior

The limbic brain, or emotional brain, is present in all animals who are born dependent on their parents for survival. This part of our brain gives us the ability to be emotionally attached to others. When we talk about feelings we are talking about the sensations and impulses that come from this part of our brain. This part of our brain also helps us to form judgments, preferences and attitudes—what we like and dislike. When we feel emotionally threatened these impulses are sent to our reptilian brain which responds in an attempt to protect us from danger.

These are some of the characteristics of the limbic brain:

1. Emotional expression

2. Social identity

3. Emotional bonding

4. Compassion and empathy

5. Happiness

6. Enjoyment of play

7. Sadness

8. Preferences, likes and dislikes

9. Sense of shame, rejection and acceptance

The neocortex, or thinking brain, features two large cerebral hemispheres. This part of our brain is able to learn and use language. The neocortex gives us the ability to organize, plan and make sense out of our emotional experiences. It helps us to use words to gain control of the nonverbal, instinctive elements of our brain—to figure out what we are thinking and feeling and what we should do about it.

These are some of the abilities of the neocortex:

1. Problem solving

2. Choosing among different options

3. Learning from our experiences

5. Using words and abstract symbols

6. Imagining things that do not exist

7. Adapting to change

If our brain team isn't working together we may overreact to stressful situations. If we only listened to our reptilian brain, we would react to any stressful situation as if we were in physical danger. If we only listened to our limbic, or emotional brain, we would always base our actions on how we are feeling at any given time. We do best when our neocortex, or thinking brain, recognizes what is going on with the other parts of our brain and takes control to make sure we respond in an appropriate way.

"The reptilian brain causes us to show ANGER when we fear we are in D-ANGER."
-The Brain Works Project

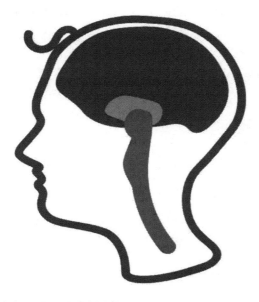

■THINKING (neocortex)

■EMOTIONAL (mammalian)

■REPTILIAN (survival)

Honesty And Coping With Upsets

Being emotionally honest means acknowledging the real reason we are upset and what we want and need. Emotional honesty is another way to solve problems starting with working things out for yourself. Often we cover up painful, upsetting feelings (recall earlier in this book secondary emotions were discussed) with feelings like anger that help us to feel stronger and less vulnerable. While this serves a purpose at times to protect us, if we are doing this *every* time we never learn how to cope with the real hurt.

Brain Works Project Director, Ronald Brill explains that humans are sensitive to four types of emotionally upsetting experiences—loss, rejection, betrayal and humiliation. Throughout the teenage years, a common source of hurt feelings is the **loss** of people in your life who have been important to you. Other losses could be the death of a pet or the loss of a physical ability due to an illness or accident. The hurt that we feel from losses helps us learn how much we really love or need what has been lost.

Rejection is the feeling that others don't like us or that we don't fit in. We can also feel rejected by those we care about when they ignore us or don't listen to us. Rejection lets us know we want to feel like we belong.

Betrayal hurts because a trust you had in another person is broken. This can happen when someone tells a secret you didn't want others to know or breaks a promise to you. The hurt we experience when we are betrayed teaches us that we need to be able to rely on and trust people.

Humiliation is an especially powerful hurt for teens because acceptance and belonging are very important at this age. Humiliation can take the form of embarrassment or shame. It may come from being laughed at or making a mistake. This feeling bothers us because we want to feel competent in what we say and do.

Emotional honesty is a way of coping with the upsetting feelings that go along with these four types of "core wounding experience." It gives you an action step for dealing with the feelings by helping you figure out what will really help you to feel better. Then you can take that information and do something effective and positive.

The next time you are upset, ask yourself the following questions:

1. What upset me?

2. Name which types of upset my experience might be called?

Loss   **Rejection**   **Betrayal**   **Humiliation**

3. What does this upset make me feel like inside? (Try to use words other than "mad," or "sad.")

4. How did this upset make me feel about myself?

5. This upset hurts since it tells me what is really important to me. What do I really want and need? What positive thing have I learned about myself?

6. What can I do about this?

Being sorry is more than saying the word. It has three parts:
1. Acknowledging that you did something you feel sorry about.
2. Telling the other person that you are sorry.
3. Showing them that you mean it by not repeating the same mistake.

Team Culture

A team's culture, or group identity, is all-important because it guides everyone's behaviors and interactions. Culture has to do with the patterns in all that we do as a team—the way we practice, the way we play and the way we socialize. Culture has to do with our attitudes, our habits, our language—our group values. Culture is a learned thing, so a new skater coming will take on the ways of thinking and acting that were established before him or her.

The Janssen Sports Leadership Center discusses different types of team cultures, some more negative or positive than others. The first step in building a great team culture is to take an honest look at your team and assess for problems.

Corrosive Culture: This type of toxic team culture has a lot of conflict, negativity, frustration, cliques, gossiping, distrust and selfishness. There is tension on and off the track. Rather than battling their opponents, this type of team spends its time battling each other or the coaches because there is little trust.

Country Club Culture: This type of team is all about appearances. There is little accountability so skaters are allowed to coast. Playing time and leadership positions are based on popularity rather than merit. Having expensive, fancy gear will earn a skater status rather than results.

Congenial Culture: This team culture is focused on getting along and having harmonious relationships. This group is more focused on being nice rather than being a high-performance team. Members might not be completely honest in their feedback to each other because they are worried about hurting feelings.

> "I love my team and they're really big butt nuggets sometimes but they're my butt nuggets."
>
> —Lucky Harms
>
> Age 13, Skating 4 years

Comfortable Culture: This team is interested in doing well but does not push itself beyond its comfort zone. This team has reasonable standards and trains to certain levels but once things get tough or uncomfortable they tend to back off. They are a moderately successful team without lifelong bonds.

Cut-Throat Culture: In this culture it is all about results, talent and success. Character and relationships are often overlooked—all that matters is winning. Team members may end up competing with each other for playing time, coaches' attention and leadership positions which can prevent or destroy relationships when taken too far. If someone is a good skater their bad attitude will be overlooked.

Championship Culture: A team with a championship culture values both relationships and results. They have a strong sense of purpose and commitment to their goals. Team members treat each other with respect and feel worthwhile no matter what their role. Team members willingly put the goals of the team above their own individual goals and take pride in being a part of something bigger than themselves.

Your team may have a combination of these types of team cultures. If your team has negative characteristics that aren't aligned with its values, it can be turned into a positive culture with very strong (mentally tough) leadership. Great cultures are built when leaders truly lead by example. Do your team captains, coaches and other leaders inspire you with actions, not just words? Great team cultures happen when leaders demonstrate that there are no rules just for others—things feel fair. Leaders can create great team cultures when they treat attitude as being just as important as skill level. Great team cultures are possible when leaders are able to keep roller derby in perspective— school, jobs, health and family always come first. Great team cultures thrive when leaders demonstrate that fulfilling the team's mission statement is more important than the points on the scoreboard—they point out the other ways to win. Leaders of great team cultures show that they may not always be able to help you achieve your roller derby goals, but they won't stop you. Great team cultures happen when leaders empower the other skaters on the team, sharing the leadership.

Six Pillars Of Character

There are six pillars of character that charactercounts.org say hold up a culture of kindness:

1. **Trustworthiness.** Be honest and don't cheat or steal. Be reliable and do what you say you will. Have the courage to do the right thing. Build a good reputation.

2. **Respect.** Be tolerant and understanding of differences. Treat yourself and others with respect. Listen to your coach and captain. Use good manners, not bad language. Be considerate of the feelings of others. Don't threaten, hit or hurt anyone (beyond what is expected in roller derby). Deal peacefully with anger, insults and disagreements

3. **Responsibility.** Do what you are supposed to even if nobody is looking. Plan ahead. Don't give up. Do your best. Think before you act. Be accountable for your words, actions and attitudes. Set a good example for others.

4. **Fairness.** Play by the rules. Take turns and share. Be open minded. Don't take advantage of others. Don't blame others carelessly. Treat all people equally.

5. **Caring.** Be kind. Show you care. Express gratitude. Forgive others. Help people in need.

6. **Citizenship.** Do your share to make your team better. Cooperate. Get involved. Stay informed. Be loyal—stand by your family, friends and your team.

> "I want to be remembered as The Butt because I'm always there. I want to be known as the all-around skater because I can skate every position. I want to be known as a confidence booster. I want people to remember me as the one that didn't get a negative attitude and brought everyone else back up."
>
> —Kick N Ash
>
> Age 16, Skating 6 years

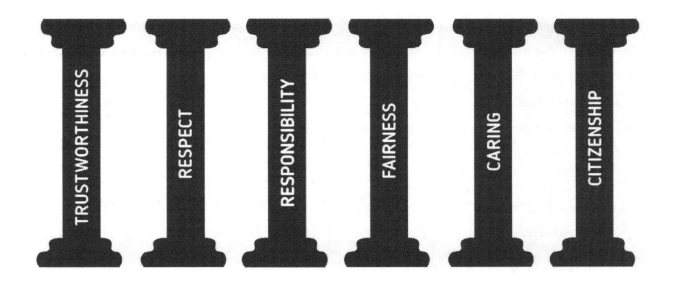

Use the Magic Ratio of 5:1, giving five compliments for each criticism.
Keep your teammates' emotional tanks filled!

Yoga For Getting Out Of Your Comfort Zone

Crane Pose (This pose is also called "Crow Pose"). Cranes were once associated with communication among people. They were said to have influenced the invention of writing with their flying formations. Cranes are associated with elegance, dignity and poise.

The crane pose builds confidence and self-awareness. This is an arm balance pose. To begin, squat down and place your hands flat on the floor about shoulder-width apart with your fingers spread wide. Keep your hands and feet where they are and lift your hips way up toward the sky. Bend your knees and lift your heels off the floor so that you are on the balls of your feet. Gently press your knees into the backs of your arms in between your elbow and your armpit. Begin to shift your weight into your fingertips, picking one foot off the floor at a time. Keep your gaze between your hands to help you balance. Try to hold the pose for a few seconds (you can definitely go longer!) and come out of the pose with control. While you are first learning the crane, set a pile of blankets or a pillow in front of you. Then if you topple forward, you won't hurt yourself.

To come into crane pose means trying something that might seem impossible at first but most can do with practice. This pose requires patience. As you are contemplating getting into crane pose or holding crane pose, think about the following:

1. What am I afraid of?
2. What does it mean to be balanced?
3. Can I remain poised no matter what I'm thinking or feeling?

You want to put everything you're learning about teambuilding into action!

What I Have Learned About Myself And My Roller Derby Performance

In each chapter of this book, you are likely to learn a variety of new things about yourself and your derby performance. After you read each chapter, complete this form as soon as possible. The purpose of this is to ensure that you are learning and remembering the important concepts from each chapter.

1._____

_____

_____

2._____

_____

_____

3._____

_____

_____

4._____

_____

_____

5._____

_____

_____

12 TEAMBUILDING ACTIVITIES

Learning mental toughness teambuilding skills will cut down on problems and strengthen the bonds you have with your teammates. Teambuilding involves understanding the similarities and differences between yourself and others and learning how to work together. This chapter is packed full of fun teambuilding activities that you can do by yourself and with your team.

Your True Colors

Are you an orange, a gold, a blue or a green? A fun way to learn how to work with the varying personalities on your team is to discover your "true colors." This method of understanding human behavior is based on Don Lowry's True Colors system and adapted into the activities below by Mary Miscisin. Categorizing people in this way is less about putting people into restrictive boxes and more about identifying what is the same and different about us, which can improve relationships. This is a great learning process to do with your whole team!

To find our which color you are, complete the True Colors Word Sort.

True Colors Word Sort

Rate the groups of words in each row from 1 to 4 according to which group you relate to the most.

4 most like you   **3** second most like you   **2** third most like you   **1** least like you

Active	Organized	Nice	Learning
Variety	Plan	Helpful	Science
Sports	Neat	Friends	Privacy
_____	_____	_____	_____

Fun	Clean	Caring	Curious
Action	On-Time	People	Ideas
Contests	Honest	Feelings	Questions
_____	_____	_____	_____

Playful	Helpful	Kind	Independent
Quick	Trustworthy	Understanding	Exploring
Adventurous	Dependable	Giving	Doing Well
_____	_____	_____	_____

Busy	Follow Rules	Sharing	Thinking
Free	Useful	Getting Along	Solving Problems
Winning	Save Money	Animals	Challenge
_____	_____	_____	_____

Exciting	Pride	Nature	Books
Lively	Tradition	Easy Going	Math
Hands-On	Do Things Right	Happy Endings	Making Sense
_____	_____	_____	_____

Totals:

| [ ] | [ ] | [ ] | [ ] |
| **ORANGE** | **GOLD** | **BLUE** | **GREEN** |

After you have totaled the ratings in each column, list your color spectrum according to which column had the highest number. The color that scored highest is your primary or dominant color.

My Color Spectrum:

1.

2.

3.

4.

You may discover that you are equally as strong in two or more colors. That is normal. Some may have rated all four colors evenly—that is normal too. All of us have all four color characteristics in our spectrums in varying amounts, however research shows most people are stronger in one group than the others.

The next section describes each color's characteristics including strengths, needs and growing edges. This information can be used to figure out ways to appreciate everyone's strong points, learn about our similarities and honor our differences. By considering what is important to the other colors, you can relate to them in such a way that they will naturally want to cooperate with you. The material can also be used to make sure our actions are aligned with how we want to be perceived. What do you need for your color to shine as brightly as possible? What do you need to do to for other colors to shine?

Blue's Strengths are accepting, communicating, creating, imagination, intuition, leading, motivating, optimism, teaching and tolerance. Blue's values are relationships and self-expression. Harmony and friendship are more important to Blue than personal victory—Blue is motivated to win when it will bring joy to his or her teammates.

> "We tend to fight but that's like we're a really big family and we're like sisters and we do get into fights but we will suck it up and figure out our differences."
>
> —Irene Yonek
>
> Age 14, Skating 5 years

Blues need you to be respectful of his or her feelings, nice, communicative, open, tolerant, genuine and accepting. Blues need to be able to express themselves and be creative. They need to have close, trusting relationships that are real. Blues like to give and receive affection. Blues have to have their feelings understood and want to find meaning in life. They value family, love, music and large social groups.

Blues are listening for the message behind the words. The best way to get a Blue to hear you is to first get to know them so there is a good relationship. Go to a Blue if you want a friend—they are great at listening!

Gold's Strengths are belonging, caretaking, responsibility, contributing, family, following directions, protecting, organizing, planning ahead, and supervising. Golds value respect, hard work and doing things the "right" way. Golds are highly reliable and make excellent leaders. To get a gold on board with your idea, tell them how it will support the team.

Golds need fairness and consistency. They feel the most comfortable when they can predict what will happen next. Golds like having their efforts recognized so give them lots of specific compliments or awards for their contributions. Golds need to be aware of who is in control and have clear expectations to follow.

Golds are listening for responsibility so they know what their part is or if the conversation is appropriate. They will hear you best if you present a well-planned, detailed conversation. Go to a Gold if you need someone who will get a project done—and it will be done well!

Orange's Strengths are being able to take charge, an ability to be carefree, dealing with chaos, determination, living in the moment, multi-tasking, negotiating, openness, risk-taking, and troubleshooting. Oranges like variety and lots of changes. They enjoy surprises and taking chances. An Orange makes a natural entertainer and like being the center of attention. Oranges don't like to wait and can make moment-to-moment decisions. They like having fun and successfully being able to live just on the safe side of "out of control."

Oranges need lots of action, activity and variety. They value winning, adventure, having choices, and honesty. You can help an Orange by giving them reminders about plans because of their natural tendency to live moment to moment. Oranges enjoy being the best and thrive on competition. With oranges be open-minded, flexible and willing to go with the flow.

Oranges are listening for an opportunity to take action and information that will be useful for them in the present or near future. Orange will hear you best if you are entertaining, relevant and keep communication

"You have to get along with everyone. Which is hard for my team because we're dramatic teenagers."

—Ginger Slap

Age 15, Skating 4 years

short and direct. Turn to an Orange if you want straight answers, fun ideas or a good laugh!

Green's Strengths are analyzing, confidence, designing, developing, inventing, mapping out, problem solving, reasoning, researching, and thinking. Greens love learning and are able to make decisions independently. Greens are big thinkers and have a drive for perfection. Greens are often misunderstood as cold and uncaring but they just don't show their emotions easily.

> "I tell myself my team loves me and believes in me so I know I can do it."
>
> —Blackheart Blockher
>
> Age 14, Skating 4 years

Greens need to know you value their wisdom and need time to think about things. Greens can be encouraged by complimenting their creativity and ability to do things well. Privacy, being challenged and new ideas are important to green. Greens value knowledge, improvement and being self-sufficient. They enjoy achieving, creative freedom, and humor.

Greens are typically listening for information and may not pay attention to extreme emotions or things that aren't interesting to them. Be prepared with facts and ready for questions when talking with a Green. Be clear with a Green if you just want them to give you empathy, rather than solving your problem. Go to a Green if you want help making a decision or need something created.

How Others May See You

Sometimes our intentions and actions are misunderstood. Traits that we view as positive in ourselves may actually be negative, irritating or off-putting to others. Think of the situations where you may not be making the impression you want to. It is important to be aware of ourselves and our effect on those around us, especially in a team environment. What can you do to make sure others can see you shine?

The other side of this coin is sometimes we misunderstand the intentions and actions of others who might not be purposely *doing things* to *try* to annoy us or come off as negative. All people are always trying to live up to their own values and fulfill their own needs—just like you! It just might not be in a way that you can easily relate to. What are some things you can do to help your teammates shine?

How Blues see themselves:

Trusting

Romantic

Polite

Caring

Nostalgic

Sympathetic

Sensitive

Flexible

How others may see Blues:

Naïve

Mushy

Groveling

Smothering

Stuck-in-the-past

Push-over

Over-emotional

Wishy-washy

How Oranges see themselves:

Carefree

Adventurous

Charming

Energetic

Bold

Impulsive

Flexible

Changing

How others may see Oranges:

Flaky

Rule Breaker

Manipulative

Uncontrollable

Obnoxious

Irresponsible

Off Task

Distracted

How Greens see themselves:

98% Right

Fair

Visionary

Intelligent

Witty

Creative

Independent

Rational

How others may see Greens:

Arrogant

Merciless

Unrealistic

Intellectual Snob

Critical

Eccentric

Anti-Social

Unfeeling

How Golds see themselves:

Stable

Conservative

Dependable

Realistic

Directive

Appropriate

Assertive

Responsible

How others may see Golds:

Rigid

Boring

Stubborn

Unimaginative

Bossy

Judgmental

Controlling

Uptight

Cory Lund Photography

"The drama is when people get mad when someone says something that's not true. And this starts this whole entire battle of 'you said this about me" and "no I didn't" and it starts this whole jibber jabber."

—Vampire Bunny

Age 11, Skating 4 years

Next are a few group activities that will improve relationships between the colors.

1. Make a group with others on your team who share your dimmest color. For example, if you scored the lowest on blue, you would group up with others who scored the lowest on blue. There will be four groups all together—one for each color. Discuss the values, joys and strengths of that color and then answer these questions:

How do I make a person with this primary color feel:

Respected?

Complimented?

Important?

When you are finished, share your answers with the other groups.

2. Form a group with others on your team who share your brightest color. Answer the following questions:

What does your color do that drives the other colors crazy?

What do the other colors do that drives your color crazy?

What does your color bring to the mix of colors?

What can you do to brighten the other colors?

When you are finished, share your answers with the other groups.

3. Group in four groups of mixed colors. Each skater will take a turn answering the following question:

If you could have one characteristic from each of the other colors what would it be and why?

Gold

Blue

Green

Orange

"Validate who you are and decide when, where and how you wish to best express yourself." —Mary Miscisin, Author of Showing Our True Colors

Back-To-Back Drawing Activity

Communication among team members is critical! Communication has two parts—sending and receiving. Sometimes we are the sender, or the one who is trying to send a message. Sometimes we are the receiver, or the one who is trying to understand the message. This team activity involves art and communication and is done in pairs. Materials needed: something to draw with (pencil, pen, marker, crayon) and some paper.

1. Break up into pairs.

2. Each person will have the drawing materials.

3. Sit back-to-back so you can't see what your partner is drawing.

4. One person will give instructions for what the other person should draw.

5. The person giving the instructions will also follow their own instructions at the same time.

6. Keep it simple such as a basic shape.

7. When you are done, turn around and compare your drawings.

8. Now switch so the other person has a turn to give instructions.

Discussion can focus on why the pictures look different or the same, any breakdowns in communication and how to improve communication.

> "I think it's great to have someone to trust and someone to rely on. If it wasn't for them I would suck at skating. Sometimes I want them to think of themselves how much I think of them."
>
> —Ally Oops
>
> Age 17, Skating 4 years

The old "count to ten before you act" advice is still good. It gives time for the initial emotional urge to fade so that you can make a value-driven decision.

Telephone Activity

This activity has been around for ages. Have your team sit in a circle. Pick one person to start. That person will whisper a message to the person next to them. The receiver of the message then whispers what they heard to the person next to them and so on until it makes its way to everyone around the circle. The person receiving the message needs to listen carefully because they can hear it only once—no repeating! The final skater says out-loud the message that they heard. This team activity can teach us many lessons including:

- **Direct communication is always best.** To ensure we are getting our messages across accurately, tell it directly to the intended person. Think about this the next time you ask someone to tell something to someone else for you.

- **Why gossip is so damaging.** Part of the reason gossip and rumors are so destructive is they end up taking on their own life as they spread.

- **How to be good listeners.** If the message that is communicated by the last person in the circle exactly matches the message that was sent out, nice job!

T.H.I.N.K before you speak:

Is it True?

Is it Helpful?

Is it Inspiring?

Is it Necessary?

Is it Kind?

3 Baskets Activity

Are you the type of person that isn't bothered by anything? Are you the type that takes issue with every single thing that comes up? It is best to find a balance between these two types of responses—not too reactionary nor too indifferent. Write down a list of all the things that upset you or bother you in roller derby. Cut them out and then put them into one of three piles which symbolize the three baskets below. To be balanced you will want to make sure you have put at least one problem in each basket.

> "I have to be able to talk to my team and be able to relate to them and get to know them on a personal level. Less distancing."
>
> —Blackheart Blockher
>
> Age 14, Skating 4 years

Basket A: These are the issues that absolutely need to be addressed. These are things you should not let slide because somebody could get hurt. Examples:

- Bullying, racism or other intolerance
- A serious health or safety issue

Basket B: These are the things that are negotiable, meaning you try to work these problems out with the others involved. It is not imperative that you 100% get your way—compromise may be the solution. Small issues that you tried to let go but are continuing to bother you also go in this category. By dealing with these Basket B's problems you are preventing them from turning into bigger ones. Examples:

- Your teammate continuously tells you what to do at practice and it is frustrating you
- Your friend seems like she's mad at you and you're worried about it.

Basket C: These are things you can let go without bringing them up. When you take everything into consideration they are not that big of a deal. That means after a short period of time these problems no longer bother you. Minor annoyances fall into this category.

Examples:

- Somebody borrows your stuff one time without asking
- A teammate hits you illegally during practice but doesn't injure you

Yoga For More Than One

Forest. Make a large circle with everyone on your team, facing in and standing about 3 feet apart. First every skater will come into Tree Pose individually, trying to hold it for five breaths, repeating the pose on both sides. Next everyone will raise both arms and stretch them out, fingers pointing up. Hands will be placed together with the person on each side of you, lifting right legs up in Tree Pose. Press into each other's hands and use each other for support. Hold for five to seven breaths. Repeat on other leg.

In a forest, groups of trees shield each other from getting knocked down by wind and link their roots for even greater support. Was it easier to balance in tree pose with the support of your teammates?

14-Day Character Building Challenge

Dare yourself to be the best person you can be with a 14-Day Character Building Challenge. Cut out each of the challenges (they can be found in the Appendix on page 207), fold them in half and put them into a jar. Select one challenge from the jar to complete every day for two weeks. You will get an opportunity to apply the Six Pillars of Character and other concepts from the teambuilding chapters with this activity. When you have accomplished all of the challenges you can put them back and start over or think of new ones. Over time, with practice, you will be able to create new habits and new ways of being that you are proud of. Take the challenge!

Your team is important to you and you are showing that through your actions.

What I Have Learned About Myself And My Roller Derby Performance

In each chapter of this book, you are likely to learn a variety of new things about yourself and your derby performance. After you read each chapter, complete this form as soon as possible. The purpose of this is to ensure that you are learning and remembering the important concepts from each chapter.

1._____

_____

_____

2._____

_____

_____

3._____

_____

_____

4._____

_____

_____

5._____

_____

_____

13 CONCLUSION

In this final chapter of *The Ultimate Mental Toughness Guide: Junior Roller Derby*, there is a short summary of some of the key concepts covered in the book. This is a review but also an opportunity for you to go back and re-read any parts you feel need extra understanding.

Cory Lund Photography

Chapter 1 Introduction

In this chapter you learned about yoga principles and worked with the book's first yoga pose.

Yoga Breathing principles

Be aware of your breath. Pay attention to how you are breathing.

Breathe through your nose. Breathe in and out (inhale and exhale) through your nose.

Slow the breath. Breathe in a slow, easy and natural way. Don't hold your breath!

Move with your breath. In yoga we coordinate our movements and our breath.

Yoga Alignment principles

Hands. When the hands are holding your weight, spread your fingers wide and press evenly through your fingertips and the four corners of your hand.

Feet. When you are standing on your feet, spread your toes and press evenly through the four corners of each foot.

Knees. When in poses where the knee is bent, be sure the knee is positioned right over the ankle.

Star Pose

Chapter 2 Goal Setting

In Chapter 2 you set a direction for your derby career by setting a goal. You used both the left and right sides of your brain with the Goal Mapping templates. You made sure your goal was S.M.A.R.T. by including the elements below. You also learned about stages of change, the power of words and ways to maximize commitment.

Specific

Measurable

Action-oriented

Realistic

Time-limited

| I can't/ I don't want to. | I might be able. to do it. | This is how to do it. | I'm doing it. | I did it! |

Words are powerful.

Warrior II Pose

Chapter 3 The MAC Approach

This was the first chapter based on the MAC approach to mental toughness:

The M in MAC stands for Mindfulness.

The A in MAC stands for Acceptance.

The C in MAC stands for Commitment.

You learned about the connection between your thoughts, feelings and actions and began to look at how certain thoughts and feelings become barriers to your best performance. You also learned about "the zone" and how this book could help increase your chances of being in the zone by helping you to be mindful, self-aware, focused on what is relevant, in the moment and confident.

Here your first mindfulness activities were introduced, the Breath Counting Exercise and the Basic Centering Exercise.

Understand the difference between motivation and commitment. Motivation is having the desire for something. Commitment is taking the steps necessary to achieve it. Motivation is nice, but commitment is necessary.

Triangle Pose

Chapter 4 Mindfulness

This chapter taught you that being mindful means being confident and fully absorbed in your activities. You learned about automatic behaviors and how mindfulness skills can help you to be the king of your inner jungle. You took the Mindfulness Attention Awareness Scale to see what level your mindfulness skills were at.

Be the lion, not the dog.

You also learned about the concept of cognitive fusion, or acting as if what our mind is telling us is the truth. The counterpart to cognitive fusion is cognitive defusion, where we can step back from all the stuff inside our heads and see it for what it really is. This allows us to have some space to imagine how we want to respond instead of reacting. You practiced two new mindfulness exercises, A Mindful Snack and A Mindful Chore.

Stimulus   ⟶   Response

Stimulus   **SPACE**⟶   Response

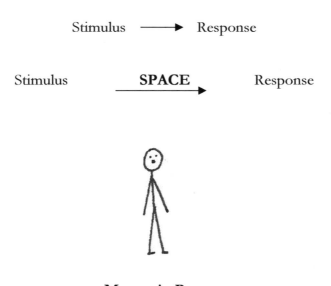

Mountain Pose

Chapter 5 Values

In Chapter 5 you determined why roller derby and your roller derby goals are important to you. You used these values to figure out what value-driven actions were necessary to live up to them. You also explored how a value-driven life differs from one where you are driven by your emotions. Next you created a list of all the emotions involved in derby, those you consider negative and those you consider positive. The What I Have Given Up For Emotions Form let you see how trying to change, control or avoid certain emotions gets in the way of you achieving your roller derby goals. This chapter also contained a new mindfulness exercise, Painting With The Breath, and you planned for your first roller derby-related mindfulness activity.

In order to make sure we are living a value-driven life,
we need to ask ourselves this question.
"Would I be acting like this if I was in a different mood?"

Tree Pose

Chapter 6 Acceptance

Chapter 6 was about beginning to have a real acceptance of all the types of thoughts and feelings that go along with roller derby, good and bad, and to learn to tolerate and co-exist with them. You learned about focusing your attention on what is relevant to the task at hand, rather than being focused on thoughts and feelings. You learned the 3-2-1 Centering Exercise which is a quick and easy way to get out of your head when needed. This chapter also reviewed how mindfulness can help us with the process of acceptance by creating distance between ourselves and our thoughts and feelings.

The concept of poise was also discussed in this chapter. You took another look at the way certain emotions can interfere with our performance by completing the Emotion and Performance Interference Form. An activity was included to help you to be able to honor all of your feelings, even if they seem conflicting. Finally, you planned to apply mindfulness to a slightly more complicated derby activity.

You need to be able to do what you need to do no matter how you are thinking or feeling—no matter what is going on in your head.
This is the ultimate definition of mental toughness.

Seated Forward Bend

Chapter 7 Commitment

This chapter was all about commitment—commitment to your goals, commitment to your values and commitment to the actions that it will take to get you there. You planned to do a different roller derby-related mindfulness activity and continue to practice mindfulness every day.

Approach, rather than avoid

Bow Pose

Chapter 8 Poise

In Chapter 8 you worked on being stronger and more flexible in response to certain thoughts and feelings. You completed a Focus Training Exercise, learned about opposite actions and made a plan for how you would respond in certain potentially upsetting situations.

Opposite Action Chart		
Emotion	**Emotion's Action Urge**	**Opposite Action**
Sad	Be alone, be quiet, not participate	Join in with others, get active
Angry	Yell, be hurtful, attack	Be extra kind, no judgments, gently avoid
Frustrated	Give up, try too hard	Keep trying, slow down
Betrayed	Hurt or revenge	Forgiveness
Worthless	Be self-destructive	Treat yourself well
Fear	Avoidance, Run away	Stay and do what is fearful
Shame	Hide	Be public

Letting go.

Eagle Pose

Chapter 9 Putting It All Together

Here you consolidated the concepts you had worked on so far in the book and put together a plan so that you would continue to keep practicing the skills after you had finished the book. You practiced several different Focus Training exercises designed to teach you to be able to shift from upsetting internal experiences to what you need to focus on externally to be successful. Last you reaffirmed your values and your commitment to whatever actions it takes to stay true to them, no matter what the situation.

Seated Twist

Chapter 10 Confidence

Chapter 10 taught you that confidence allows you to take the actions necessary to fulfill your dreams. This chapter contained several confidence building activities including a visualization and four yoga poses.

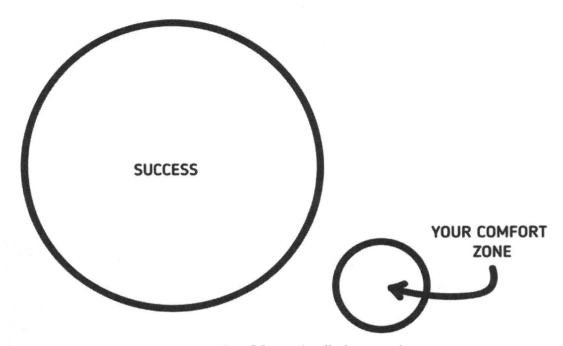

Confidence is all about action.

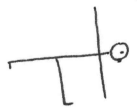

Half-Moon Pose

Plank Pose

Downward Dog

Crescent Lunge

Chapter 11 The Science Of Teambuilding

This was the first of *two* chapters on teambuilding because this area is super important. Included here was information on sportsmanship (sports-person-ship), communication, problem solving and conflict resolution. You also learned about the three parts of the brain—the reptilian, the limbic and the neocortex, and how they need to work together for us to be able to deal with stressful situations. Emotional honesty was taught as a way to cope by working things out with yourself. When we understand what we really need, we can put that information into effective and positive actions. Then you learned about the different types of team cultures, what it takes to change yours if needed and the Six Pillars of Character. Phew, that was a big chapter!

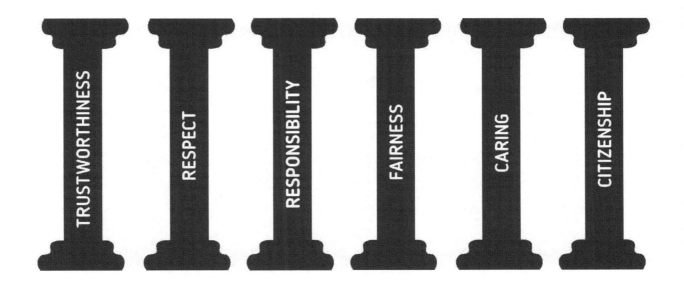

Seek first to understand.

Crane Pose

Chapter 12 Teambuilding Activities

The second chapter on teambuilding was full of activities that you could do on your own and with your team. The True Colors activity was a fun way to get to know yourself and learn how to work with different personalities. The chapter ended with a 14-Day Character Building challenge so you could put many of the concepts from this book into action.

Gold

Blue

Green

Orange

Forest

"Validate who you are and decide when, where and how you wish to best express yourself (2010, pg. 33 Miscisin, M.)."

Lydia Brewer Photography

In Conclusion

This part of your journey to mental toughness is almost complete. Below is the Mental Toughness Quiz you took in the first chapter of this book. Take it again and see how your scores have improved!

> "I hope I don't break a leg any time soon."
>
> —Tap Out
>
> Age 13, Skating 3 ½ years

Mental Toughness Quiz

1	2	3	4	5
Not at all	A little bit	Somewhat	Mostly	Definitely!

____ I know what mental toughness is.

____ I know why I play roller derby.

____ My roller derby goals are clear.

____I am aware of my thoughts, feelings and actions.

____ I am in the present moment when I perform.

____ I notice when my focus is not where it needs to be.

____ I am able to shift my attention to where it needs to be to perform my best.

____ I accept that I will sometimes have negative thoughts and feelings on the way to achieving my derby goals.

____ I can choose how I respond to my thoughts and feelings.

____ My actions are in line with my values (what is important to me).

____ I am committed to doing what it takes to perform at my best.

____ I am confident.

____ I am a great teammate.

Scoring:

1-19 You are just starting on your mental toughness journey.

20-49 You have some mental toughness skills.

50-65 You are mentally tough!

"I want people to think of my team name and think of me and something great that I did, like a particular jam or something like how I go that and spun around on one foot and didn't fall or give up. I think everyone wants to be remembered. I want to have a good impact on roller derby."

—Slim Reaper

Age 16, Skating 7 years

Yoga For Looking Ahead

Cobra Pose. The figure of the serpent has symbolized the power that is within each individual. The shedding of skin is seen to represent transformation and renewal. Many people are afraid of snakes. When a snake's head moves, the movement is transmitted all the way through its body to the tail.

Lie on your belly with the tops of your feet on the floor and legs close together. Place your palms flat on the floor under your shoulders. Your fingers will be pointing straight ahead. Press into the four corners of your hands. Inhale and lift your head, heart and belly. Keep your shoulders back and down, elbows close to the body and the tops of your feet on the floor. Your eyes look up. Hold for two breaths, lower slowly and repeat two more times.

As you work with Cobra Pose, reflect on the following questions:

1. How can I shed my old skin?
2. Am I leading with my head?
3. Where does my power come from?

Hopefully you have enjoyed reading the *Ultimate Toughness Guide: Junior Roller Derby*. This was a long, but worthwhile journey towards mental toughness. The skills in this book aren't meant to be left here on these pages, but taken out and incorporated into all aspects of your life—roller derby and beyond!

Remember to enjoy the ride.

ADDENDUM: FOR PARENTS

So far this whole book has been dedicated to you, the junior roller derby skater. This chapter is written for your parents or other caregivers for the purpose of providing a few tips to help them motivate and empower you. If they are not reading this book along with you, please let your parents know there is a chapter just for them. Of course, you are welcome to read this chapter too!

Dear roller derby parent:
Thank you for supporting your skater's participation in this crazy-awesome-amazing sport. It shows you care about them being active, social, and having the opportunity to learn and grow in areas such as confidence, fitness and leadership. You do it all—you transport your kid to practice and to games. You pay for gear and extra training opportunities. You host sleepovers for their teammates who have become an extension of your own family. You help by doing everything from sitting on the Board to baking cupcakes for the latest fundraiser. Supporting your kid's roller derby career not only enriches their life but ensures that derby is available as a positive outlet and safe refuge for future youth.
This chapter is meant to provide information on ways for you to enhance your support of your child and to help ensure that they are getting all of the benefits they can out of roller derby.

Why Roller Derby?

Why does your child want to play roller derby? Some parents have never asked their child this question. In Chapter 5 they completed exercises to determine what was important to them about derby and to identify what their values were behind those things. Values are the guiding force behind any actions or decisions we make. Your skater's value-driven actions will take them in the direction of their roller derby goals and help them to act in the service of what is truly important to them. To define your vision as a roller derby parent, take the following steps:

1. Define the values that are most important to you and that you want to see in your child.

2. List the life lessons you hope you kid will learn from roller derby.

3. Form a vision of your future child.

4. Ask yourself, *Are my actions leading toward my vision, or something entirely different?*

"My family loves derby. My sister plays and we love playing together. She always expects me to make her a hole. We always go to practice. My mom is very supportive. She pushed me til I found my roots. My dad is always there and is like a second dad to the girls on the team."

—Ginger Slap

Age 15, Skating 4 years

According to John O'Sullivan's book, Changing The Game, maximum performance depends on all of these components, some of which can be influenced and some which can't:

Talent + State of Mind + Coaching + Deliberate Practice + Luck = Performance

O'Sullivan's book gives these reasons why kids say they play sports:

- To have fun
- To do something I am good at
- To improve my skills
- To get exercise and stay in shape
- To be part of a team
- Excitement of competition

Maximizing Motivation Through Empowerment

One of the challenges to being a sports parent is knowing when to push and how hard. There are times when your kid needs an extra push from you to get them moving in the direction of their roller derby goals. There are other instances when there may be a serious issue that is creating the lack of motivation or resistance. Are the tears from hurt feelings or from an injury? Do they want to skip practice because they are tired or because they are being bullied? As parents, we push because we want what is best for our kids. We want them to experience success and have pride in their accomplishments. We want them to be happy, healthy and have fun along the way. The problem with pushing or pulling is it can create resistance. If we push too hard we will get push-back. This can happen when we are more attached to the outcome than our children are.

This chapter presents an alternative to pushing as a way to motivate your skater. That alternative is motivation through self-determination and empowerment!

One of the most popular responses when parents are asked why they have their child in derby is to give them a sense of empowerment. What exactly does empowerment mean? The National Empowerment Center broke down this complex term into elements including these:

- Having decision making power
- Having access to information and resources
- Assertiveness
- Having a positive self-image
- A feeling that you can make a difference

In roller derby, having decision making power can mean allowing kids to have a say in decisions that affect themselves and their team. Parents and coaches can allow a wide range of options from which to make choices rather than just requiring a 'yes' or 'no' answer. Parents and coaches can provide education and training so that skaters can have knowledge to help them make informed decisions about things such as gear, health and safety. Avoid stepping in to act as middle man for your kid when he or she has a conflict with coaches or a teammate. Learning how to be appropriately assertive is a good skill for children to have—it can help them deal with peer pressure, bullying and more. Roller derby can help youth to be able to appreciate his or her strengths and learn how to bring them out. When your child has a positive experience on and off the track, notes their progress and feels confident in their abilities—they are empowered.

There are only three things you can do while watching your kid's game—be a coach, be an official, be a fan— and you should only be one of these at a time.

Photo by Diane Palmer

Roadblocks To Communication

When trying to motivate your kids, Thomas Gordon lists 12 roadblocks. These barriers to effective communication get in the way of your skater feeling heard and understood and can cause resistance or rebelliousness and move them further away from where they would like to go. These types of response aren't all necessarily bad, but they get in the way of good listening and interrupt your child's own exploration.

1. **Ordering, directing, commanding.** A direction is given with the force of authority behind it.

Don't say that.

You need to apologize.

Stop complaining!

2. **Warning, threatening.** These messages carry the threat that there will be negative consequences if the direction isn't followed.

If you don't start treating her better, you're going to lose her as a friend

You'd better get your act together or you won't make the travel team.

3. **Giving advice, making suggestions, providing solutions.** This is where the parent draws on his/her own knowledge and experience to recommend what their kid should do.

What I would do is…

Why don't you…

Have you tried…

4. **Persuading, arguing, lecturing.** There is an assumption here that your child has not adequately thought this through and needs help doing so.

The facts are…

Yes, but…

Actually…

5. **Moralizing, preaching.** "Should" language implies an underlying moral code. This is telling your kid the proper thing to do.

You should…

It will be good for you…

I can't believe you think that's okay!

6. **Judging, criticizing, disagreeing, blaming.** The implication here is that there is something wrong with your child or what they have said.

It's your own fault.

You're being too selfish.

I can't believe you didn't know better.

7. **Agreeing, approving, praising.** It may be surprising to find this category in the roadblocks. This kind of message gives the message that approval is needed to what has been said. True listening is different from approving.

I think you're absolutely right.

That's exactly what I would do!

You're a good kid.

8. **Shaming, ridiculing, labeling, name-calling.** These messages of disapproval are directed at shaming or correcting a certain attitude or behavior.

That's really stupid.

You should be ashamed of yourself.

You're being a brat.

9. **Interpreting, analyzing.** This is a very common and tempting one for those who want to seek out the hidden meaning in your kid's statements and provide your own interpretation.

You don't really mean that.

Do you know what your real problem is…?

10. **Reassuring, sympathizing, consoling.** The intent here is to make your child or yourself feel better. There isn't necessarily anything bad about this, but it's not listening.

It's going to be okay.

You'll be fine.

Don't worry.

11. **Questioning, probing.** People often think asking questions make them a good listener. Questions interfere with the spontaneous flow of communication, diverting it in the directions that interest you, but may not concern your child.

> "My mom is the one who got me into derby. She started derby with me and that was really really fun because I got to hang out with my mom. We were in fresh meat together. My mom really supports me."
>
> —Ally Oops
>
> Age 17, Skating 4 years

> "My parents are always trying to get me here on time or take me to extra things that will help me improve. I get praised by everyone in my family because they find it rare. My family has all been to my games and they really enjoy seeing it."
>
> —Brozilla
>
> Age 16, Skating 2 ½ years

Why are you doing that?

Doesn't that make you mad?

Why didn't you…?

12. **Withdrawing, distracting, humoring, changing the subject.** This roadblock attempts to get your kid's mind off it. It gives the message that what your kid was talking about should not be pursued.

Let's talk about something happy.

That reminds me of a time I…

Seems like you got up on the wrong side of the bed today.

The take away from this section is there is a time for teaching and advice giving and there is a time for listening or responding in a way that encourages your child's own discovery. It can be tough because we really want what is best for our kids or to take away their pain. As a parent of teens, it takes patience to merely plant seeds and then sit back and wait for them to grow.

Practice listening to your skater without arguing, correcting, questioning or judging. For one minute just let them talk while you listen.

Empower Your Kid With Reflective Statements

 To make your child feel heard and understood and to facilitate their own growth processes, use reflective statements instead of the roadblocks above. A reflective statement tells your skater that you understand how they are feeling and what it is they want or need. Reflective statements cue your skater to take actions that are in line with what is truly important to them. Reflective statements are also great because if you do them well you are really just holding a mirror up to your child so they can work things out with themselves. This reduces arguing and power struggles between the two of you. You are allowing them to feel empowered and to be able to make decisions that reflect their values. Below are some things your child might say to you, a potential roadblock to communication, and a reflective statement which can guide your child back to making a choice that is in the service of their values.

Kid: *My coach hates me! She knew I wanted to skate in the last jam.*

Parent response with roadblock: *Calm down! It's not a big deal. There's always next time.*

Parent response with reflective statement: *You're feeling mad at your coach. You wanted to go out in that last to show her what you could do.* This reflects the kid's core value of accomplishment or notoriety.

Kid: *I'm too tired to go to practice tonight.*

Parent response with roadblock: *You have to go; your teammates are counting on you.*

Parent response with reflective statement: *Relaxing at home is important to you, but so is your commitment to your team.* This reflects the kid's core value of hard work or integrity.

Kid: *I can't stand the drama! Everyone always spreads rumors about everyone else!*

Parent response with roadblock: *Just ignore it.*

Parent response with reflective statement: *You're frustrated with how the other girls are acting. Being a loyal friend is important to you.* This reflects the kid's core value of loyalty or peace.

It can take up to 20 minutes to fully calm after a meltdown.
Your kid loses the ability to reason while upset. This is not the time to teach.

The Recency Effect

The Recency Effect describes a phenomenon where the last thing a person hears is the thing they remember best and respond to. Try rearranging your statements to your child so that the direction you want them to take and what you want them to respond to is at the end. This effect becomes even more apparent when a person hears long instructions or lists of things.

For example, if you tell your skater, "Please wash your gear, it really stinks!" You kid will likely respond to the stinky part saying something like, "No it doesn't!" or "It doesn't stink as bad as so-and-so on my team."

If you switch the order of your statement to "Your gear really stinks, please wash it." Then your kid will respond to the washing part saying something like, "Ok I will after school tomorrow." Or they may not agree to wash it, but at least you will be having a discussion in a productive direction.

Here are some more examples:

Instead of "Talk to the coach if you feel you are being treated unfairly." Here the child will respond to the unfairness of the situation.

Try "If you feel you are being treated unfairly you need to talk to the coach about this." In this order, your child will respond to doing something about his or her situation.

Instead of "You wish there was a way you could get the other kids on your team to treat your teammate better. That sounds really frustrating." With the statements in this order, your child will respond to feeling frustrated.

Try "That sounds really frustrating. You wish there was a way you could get the other kids on your team to treat your teammate better." By flipping the order of the statements, your skater can focus on taking action.

10 Rules For Sports Parents

1. **Let the coach do their job!** During games and practices, your kid should only be listening to instructions from their coaches. You are there as a spectator and a cheerleader. If you start telling your child what to do, the coach's authority is undermined and it puts your kid in the difficult and confusing situation of trying to decide who to listen to.

2. **Don't live your dreams through your kids.** It is healthy and natural to want your kids to do well. Sometimes parents over-identify with their children and their success or failure becomes the parents' success or failure. In these extreme cases, if the child does not succeed, the parent's self-image is threatened.

3. **React to process and progress.** If you are only giving big reactions to big accomplishments or big plays you are giving your skater the message that only outcomes are important. Instead, demonstrate to your child that their whole sports journey is valuable. Focus praise on processes such as focus and commitment in addition to individual improvement. Never make comparisons between your child and other skaters.

> "When I need new elbow pads and knee pads they get them for me because they're worried about my safety. When I have good stuff I won't get hurt."
>
> —Vampire Bunny
>
> Age 11, Skating 4 years

200

4. **Make your expectations for your child clear.** Tell your skater what you expect—like giving maximum effort, playing fair, listening to their coach and having fun. This will help avoid any misunderstandings your kid might have about what you expect out of them—they might think you want them to be the best or always win.

5. **Cheer for everyone.** Of course you are going to cheer for you own kid when they do well, but don't forget to cheer for everyone else on the team too. Your child is part of a team and that whole team deserves your support, win or lose. Cheer for great plays by skaters on the opposing team as well. Never put the opponent down to make your kid feel good.

6. **Be a role model.** Treat all officials, coaches, parents, fans and skaters with respect. It is your duty to show your skater what good sportsmanship looks like. If you have a problem with the coach talk to them in private after the game or practice. You can't hold your kid to standards you don't adhere to. As attachment researcher, Kent Hoffman says, a parent should always be bigger, stronger, wiser and kind.

7. **Leave your kid alone on the ride home after games.** This is a time when emotions are high—disappointment, frustration and exhaustion are heightened for both you and your kid. Trying to turn this time into a teachable moment can make your kid feel as though their worth is tied to their athletic performance and the wins or losses of the team. Give them the time and space to digest the game and recover physically and emotionally. When your child is ready to talk, be a quiet and reflective listener.

8. **Make it safe to make mistakes.** Help your skater see failure as part of the learning process rather than something to be avoided. Instead of fearing failure, your kid will learn to embrace and overcome challenges. Never see your child's sport as a financial investment needing a return in great performance. Give your kid the room to grow, but stay by their side and help them grow up.

9. **Remember why your kid is doing this.** The number one reason kids want to play junior roller derby is to have FUN! Kids play in sports because they are *play* and they drop out when they stop being fun. Help your skater balance derby with other aspects of their life such as school, family and social life. Keep things in perspective.

10. **Tell your kid, "I love to watch you play."** Say this after every game, every time and really mean it. Don't treat your child differently depending on game outcome. This will show your child that you feel proud of them and love them unconditionally.

Family Roller Derby Mission Statement

Work with your skater to create a Family Roller Derby Mission Statement. First, ask your kid why they play roller derby. Next, ask them how coaches and parents can make derby more enjoyable. Then, ask your child what coaches and parents do that make derby less enjoyable. Take your child's answers and come up with your mission statement. You can include things like:

- Purpose of sports
- Values that are important to your family
- The reasons your child plays
- The ways the adults help your kid enjoy roller derby
- The things to avoid that make roller derby less enjoyable

Keep lectures to 25 words or less! This will allow you to focus on the key points you want to make and guarantee your child will take it all in.

loVe

As parents, we want to support our kids in a way that will allow them to gradually make the transition to responsible adulthood. The parenting journey can be conceptualized as the shape of a letter 'V' which is narrower at the bottom and wider at the top. When our children are smaller we need to keep a tighter grasp on them—they get small choices. It is necessary for safety reasons for our kids to make fewer decisions and have less freedom. As our children grow older, it is important that we loosen our control over them and give them the opportunity to make more decisions for themselves—they get big choices! They need to experience increasing freedom and the responsibility that goes along with it. Let your kids have the opportunity to make some mistakes and bad decisions while you are there as a safety net.

loVe

> "My dad gives me opportunities."
>
> —Irene Yonek
>
> Age 16, Skating 5 years

APPENDIX

Photo by Dani Hubbard

A FEW ALTERNATE STORIES FOR FOCUS TRAINING EXERCISES

The Cat, the Rooster, and the Young Mouse

An Aesop Fable

A very young mouse made his first trip out of the hole and into the world. He returned to tell his mother of the wonderful creatures he saw.

"Oh, Mother," said the mouse, "I saw some curious animals. There was one beautiful animal with fluffy fur and a long winding tail. She made such a tender vibrating noise. I saw another animal, a terrible looking monster. He had raw meat on his head and on his chin that wiggled and shook as he walked. He spread out his sides and cried with such a powerful and frightening wail, that I scurried away in fear, without even talking to the kind beautiful animal.

Mother Mouse smiled, "My dear, that horrible creature was a harmless bird, but that beautiful animal with the fluffy fur was a mouse-eating cat. You are lucky she did not have you for dinner."

Do not trust outward appearances.

The Frog and the Ox

An Aesop Fable

One afternoon a grand and wonderful ox was on his daily stroll, when he was noticed by a small haggardly frog. The frog was too impressed with the great ox, impressed to the point of envy.

"Look at this magnificent ox!" he called to all his friends, "He's such a grand size for an animal, but he's no greater than I am if I tried."

The frog started puffing and swelled from his normal size.

"Am I as large as the wonderful ox?" he asked his friends.

"No, no, not near as grand as the ox," they replied.

So, the frog puffed himself up more and more, trying to reach the state of the ox.

"Now? Now?" asked the frog.

"No, no. But please, don't try anymore," pleaded his friends.

But the frog continued to puff and swell, larger and larger until he finally burst.

Be true to your own character.

The Rooster and the Fox
An Aesop Fable

A rooster was perched on a branch of a very high tree, crowing loudly. His powerful exclamations were heard throughout the forest and caught the attention of a hungry fox who was out and about looking for a prey.

The fox saw how high the bird was positioned and thought of a sly way to bring the rooster down for his meal.

"Excuse me, my dear proud Rooster," he gently spoke, "Have you not heard of the universal treaty and proclamation of harmony that is now set before all beasts and birds and every creature in our forest. We are no longer to hunt or prey nor ravish one another, but we are to live together in peace, harmony, and love. Do come down, Rooster, and we shall speak more on this matter of such great importance."

Now, the rooster, who knew that the fox was known for his sly wit, said nothing, but looked out in the distance, as if he were seeing something.

"At what are you looking so intently?" asked the fox.

"I see a pack of wild dogs," said the rooster, "I do believe they're coming our way, Mr. Fox."

"Oh, I must go," said the fox.

"Please do not go yet, Mr. Fox," said the rooster, "I was just on my way down. We will wait on the dogs and discuss this new time of peace with all."

"No, no," said the fox, "I must go. The dogs have not heard of this treaty of peace yet."

Beware of the sudden offers of friendship.

14-Day Character Building Challenge

	For one whole day be honest. Don't lie or or exaggerate.	Don't speak negatively about others today. If friends start to gossip around you, walk away.	If you owe someone an apology, today is the day to say you're sorry.
Listen for compliments today and simply say, "Thank you." A compliment is a gift--take it!	Try to learn one thing today from someone who irritates you.	Instead of taking yourself too seriously, laugh at yourself if you make a mistake today.	Let the other person be right today.
If there is someone who has been trying to break into your group of friends, open your heart and let them in today.	Today, only agree to things you plan to follow through on.	Think of something or someone you are grateful for. Show your gratitude today.	Look for someone who could use some help today and offer to help them.
Think of someone who offended you recently and surprise them by treating unkindness with kindness.	Do more listening than talking today.	Do your absolute best today with everything you do, from chores to homework.	

REFERENCES

5 Rules for Youth Sports Parents. Retrieved July 13, 2016, from
http://newsblog.sportssignup.com/blog/bid/120929/5-Rules-for-Youth-Sports-Parents

5 Yoga Poses for Confidence and Inner Strength. (2014). Retrieved July 13, 2016, from
http://www.doyouyoga.com/5-yoga-poses-for-confidence-and-inner-strength/

10 Heartwarming Stories Of Sportsmanship To Brighten Your Day. Retrieved July 13, 2016,
from https://www.buzzfeed.com/jpmoore/the-10-most-heartwarming-moments-of-
sportsmanship?utm_term=.hhBNPe2Qa#.hsB5p7Xqx

10 Strong-Core Yoga Poses to Build Confidence: Baptiste Yoga Sequence. (2015). Retrieved July
13, 2016, from http://www.yogajournal.com/slideshow/core-strengthening-poses-build-
confidence/

Basics of Communication. Retrieved July 13, 2016, from
https://www.psychologytoday.com/blog/notes-self/201307/basics-communication

The Brain From Top to Bottom. Retrieved July 13, 2016, from
http://thebrain.mcgill.ca/flash/d/d_05/d_05_cr/d_05_cr_her/d_05_cr_her.html

Center for Adolescent Studies. Retrieved July 13, 2016, from
http://centerforadolescentstudies.com

Confidence Activities. Retrieved July 13, 2016, from https://www.polk-fl.net/

Confidence VS Self-Esteem: The Confidence Code. (2014). Retrieved July 13, 2016, from http://theconfidencecode.com/2014/03/confidence-vs-self-esteem/

Coping Skills & Tools. Retrieved July 13, 2016, from

http://www.copingskills4kids.net/Coping_Skills___Tools.html

Covey, S. (n.d.). The 7 habits of highly effective teens: The ultimate teenage success guide.

Do You Know What Your Core Really Is and What it Does? Retrieved July 13, 2016, from

http://breakingmuscle.com/mobility-recovery/do-you-know-what-your-core-really-is-and-what-it-does

Facts For Teens: Conflict Resolution. Retrieved July 13, 2016, from http://herkimercounty.org/

Five Great Moments of Sportsmanship in 2014. Retrieved July 13, 2016, from

http://www.sikids.com/si-kids/2016/01/12/year-sportsmanship

Gardner, F. L., & Moore, Z. E. (2007). The psychology of enhancing human performance: The mindfulness-acceptance-commitment (MAC) approach. New York: Springer Pub.Gillen, L., &

Gillen, J. (2007). Yoga calm for children: Educating heart, mind, and body. Portland, OR: Three Pebble Press.

Harwood, C. G., & Knight, C. J. (2016). Parenting in sport. Sport, Exercise, and Performance Psychology, 5(2), 84-88. doi:10.1037/spy0000063

How Can I Improve My Self-Esteem? Retrieved July 13, 2016, from

http://kidshealth.org/en/teens/self-esteem.html

How to Be a Good Sport. Retrieved July 13, 2016, from http://kidshealth.org/en/kids/good-sport.html#

The Importance of Effective Communication. Retrieved July 13, 2016, from

https://ysrinfo.files.wordpress.com/2012/06/effectivecommunication5.pdf

JRDA Code of Conduct. Retrieved July 13, 2016, from http://www.juniorrollerderby.org/rules

Life and Work. Retrieved July 13, 2016, from http://www.viktorfrankl.org/e/lifeandwork.html

Miscisin, M. (2001). Showing our true colors: A fun, easy guide for understanding and appreciating yourself and others. Riverside, CA: True Colors.

Naar-King, S., & Suarez, M. (2011). Motivational Interviewing With Adolescents and Young Adults. New York: Guilford Press.

National Empowerment Center. Retrieved July 13, 2016, from

https://www.power2u.org/articles/empower/working_def.html

O'Sullivan, J. (2014.). Changing the Game: The parent's guide to raising happy, high-performing athletes and giving youth sports back to our kids.

Prochaska, J. & Velicer, W. (n.d.) The Transtheoretical Model of Health Behavior Change. Retrieved July 13, 2016, from http://luci.ics.uci.edu/websiteContent/weAreLuci/biographies/faculty/djp3/LocalCopy/prochaska.pdf

The Real-world Benefits of Strengthening Your Core. Retrieved July 13, 2016, from http://www.health.harvard.edu/healthbeat/the-real-world-benefits-of-strengthening-your-core

Self-Esteem Activities for Children, Teens, and Young Adults. (2014). Retrieved July 13, 2016, from http://www.kimscounselingcorner.com/2014/06/01/self-esteem/

Selected Self-Confidence Building Activities. Retrieved July 13, 2016, from http://www.uncommonhelp.me/articles/selected-self-confidence-building-activities/

The Six Pillars of Character. Retrieved July 13, 2016, from https://charactercounts.org/program-overview/six-pillars/

The 7 C's That Will Help You Communicate Better. Retrieved July 13, 2016, from http://www.inc.com/peter-economy/the-7-c-s-that-will-help-you-communicate-better.html

Types of Communication: Verbal, Written, and Nonverbal. Retrieved July 13, 2016, from https://www.boundless.com/management/textbooks/boundless-management-textbook/communication-11/understanding-communication-82/types-of-communication-verbal-written-and-nonverbal-396-1385/

Youth Soccer Insider: The Ride Home: Not a Teachable Moment. Retrieved July 13, 2016, from http://www.socceramerica.com/article/53127/the-ride-home-not-a-teachable-moment.html

Understanding the Eight Kinds of Team Cultures. Retrieved July 13, 2016, from https://coachad.com/articles/understanding-the-eight-kinds-of-team-cultures/

Value Card Set. Retrieved July 13, 2016, from http://www.uihi.org/

Viegas, M. (2004). Relax Kids: Aladdin's magic carpet and other fairy tale meditations for children. Alresford: O Books.

Want a Great Team, Build a Great Culture. Retrieved July 13, 2016, from http://www.forbes.com/sites/sanjeevagrawal/2015/10/05/want-a-great-team-build-a-great-culture/#1541055652da

Weitz, N. (2014). The Ultimate Mental Toughness Guide: Roller derby. Createspace Publishing.

What is Character? Retrieved July 13, 2016, from http://www.character-training.com/blog/

What is the Power of Positive? Retrieved July 13, 2016, from http://www.positivecoach.org/the-power-of-positive/

What Kind of Culture Do You Have? Discover the 8 Kinds of Cultures. Retrieved July 13, 2016, from http://www.janssensportsleadership.com/resources/janssen-blog/what-kind-of-culture-do-you-have-discover-the-7-kinds-of-cultures/

Youth Sports 101: Top 9 Tips for Moms and Dads. Retrieved July 13, 2016, from https://www.psychologytoday.com/blog/coaching-and-parenting-young-athletes/201304/youth-sports-101-top-9-tips-moms-and-dads

ABOUT THE AUTHOR

Naomi "Sweetart" Weitz has been coaching and playing roller derby since 2006. She was one of the very first derby girls in the entire Inland Northwest, founding the Spokannibals in 2010 and acting as Tournament Director for Spokarnage: A Killer Roller Derby Tournament. Sweetart has a Master's Degree in Psychology, is a Licensed Mental Health Counselor, is Certified in Sports and Fitness Psychology and is Certified as a Youth Instructor for Yoga Calm. She is the author of the Ultimate Mental Toughness Guide: Roller Derby.

ABOUT THE DESIGNER

Skyler Dean Weitz is currently studying Graphic Design at Spokane Falls Community College. He enjoys designing magazines and posters and creating music.